# PIVOTAL MOMENTS

## Memoirs from Boomer Women

Adventures
Losses
Challenges
Triumphs

*Marilyn Hamilton, Liz Helgerson,*
*Myra Lathrop, Eileen O'Grady, Martha Staib,*
*Shirley Summers, Linda Zirk*

# Dedication

To those who touched our lives and encouraged our stories—
and to all women who face the challenges in their lives
with strength, compassion, and resilience.

# Contributors

*Marilyn Hamilton* grew up in Arcadia, a city in the San Gabriel Valley area of Los Angeles in a family of four. She received a bachelor's degree in social science from San Jose State University and a Master's in Education, Counseling and Guidance from Cal Poly, San Luis Obispo, as a returning student. Her graduate degree led to a career in counseling, specializing in victims of crime. In 1980 she and her husband moved to the Central California Coast. In retirement, she enjoys piano lessons, aqua aerobics, tai chi, reading, writing, and long walks with friends.

*Liz Helgerson* compares her life to a prism with many facets, reflecting moments of bright happiness. somber loss, and pastel contentment. Despite marrying young, she completed a Ph.D. in French, discovering feminist activism along the way. As a divorced single mother, she taught French at a small college before pursuing a second career in computer systems analysis and design. She found love at the age of 50 and left her position as V.P. of a small technology company to become an oft-traveling consultant. This period ended happily with her retirement in Atascadero, California, where she stays alive intellectually with her AAUW friends.

*Myra Lathrop* is from the Los Angeles area. She graduated from U.C.L.A. with a bachelor's degree in anthropology and an M.A. in dance therapy. Dance and writing are her passions. She taught and performed salsa and has participated in aerobic dance for over 40 years. She also writes and has published her poetry and essays. In 2020 she created a collection of personal essays about life during the pandemic. After retiring to the Central Coast in 2008, she continues to dance, write, volunteer, and enjoy the beauty of this area.

*Eileen O'Grady* treasures the friendships she made in Chicago where she grew up and attended Loyola University. As a young mother, she taught classes in writing and literature at a suburban Kansas City high school. After completing her Master's degree, she also conducted workshops for teachers at the University of Missouri in Kansas City and published articles about the teaching of writing. She moved to the Central

Coast of California when she retired. She leads writing workshops and works on local political campaigns. She especially enjoys the camaraderie of the Atascadero AAUW memoir-writing group.

*Martha Staib* grew up in Oakland, California. As a senior in high school, she wrote for the school newspaper and published a weekly column in the *Oakland Times*. She received a bachelor's degree from the University of California at Davis and a Master of Medical Science in Dietetics from Emory University in Atlanta, Georgia. After returning to California in 1987, she moved to the Central Coast where she worked at a state hospital for 27 years. She also served in the U.S. Army Reserves from 1990-1998. She is now retired and spends her time learning to play the piano, creating homemade quilts, and writing with the AAUW memoir-writing group.

*Shirley Summers* describes herself as a woman whose life evolved due to opportunities she seized. Although her parents did not prepare her for college, she now holds a Master's degree and enjoyed a satisfying career as a Licensed Clinical Social Worker. She looks forward to further adventures as she travels life's path, following the one lesson she always remembers being taught: if you discover a talent, you have an obligation to develop it and use it.

*Linda Zirk* was a child of the post-WW II era who grew up in southwest London. She attended an all-girls school through the equivalent of Grade 11 and graduated with certifications in secretarial studies. After a work-study program at Kingston Technical College, she completed an associate degree in business administration. Linda relocated to New York City and then to San Francisco where she met her husband. After living in Indiana and Sacramento, they worked in the Bay Area for 25 years. They now enjoy the SLO Life on the Central Coast where Linda joined the local AAUW branch and met a fabulous group of memoir writers!

# Introduction

## About the Group:

We began to meet monthly in the fall of 2015. We knew we had stories to tell about obstacles we had overcome, losses we had suffered, unexpected victories. Each month we wrote focused memoirs about childhood events, important people in our lives—moments when we made important decisions.

We discovered that the process of writing often surprises and delights the writer. We revisited challenges we had faced and overcome—and those we still lived with. We asked ourselves what the special moments in our lives had meant. How did we decide to open one door and close another? And what happened as a result? We listened to each other; we responded; we celebrated. A receptive, supportive audience and monthly deadlines motivated us to continue.

All of us live on the Central Coast of California; most are baby boomers. Our concerns about equity for women led each of us to join the Atascadero branch of AAUW, the American Association of University Women. As AAUW members, we discovered that we also shared a common interest in writing about significant events in our lives.

During the 2020 pandemic, we decided to revise some of our drafts and create this collection, so we could share our pivotal moments with a wider audience.

## About the Facilitator:

I always loved to read and to write. I earned a bachelor's degree in English and later a Master's in education with emphasis on the teaching of writing. During my professional career, I taught English at a public high school in suburban Kansas City. I encouraged my students to brainstorm ideas, create drafts, receive feedback, and revise their work. As a National Writing Project facilitator, I also led workshops for other teachers. Whether my students were teens or other adults, I wanted them to learn that writing well empowers them.

When I retired and moved to San Luis Obispo County, I attended classes in memoir-writing at Cuesta College, participated in writing groups, and led workshops for other adults. When this AAUW-based group formed in 2015, I discovered the most dedicated and delightful group of writers I have ever known.

On behalf of all of us, I invite you to read our selections and reflect on the pivotal moments in your life. We hope our stories will inspire you to transform your memories into memoirs.

*Eileen O'Grady*

---

***Please note:*** some of the writers have changed the names of people in their memoirs to protect their identities.

# Table of Contents

# Triumphs

# Adventures

"The purpose of life, after all, is to live it, to taste experience to the utmost, to reach out eagerly and without fear for a newer and richer experience."

---

*Eleanor Roosevelt*

# A Boy from East L.A.

*By Myra Lathrop*

Alex Lopez still haunts my thoughts and dreams. I can picture him at age twelve: jet black hair slicked back with Tres Flores pomade, wearing a bright white T-shirt under a Pendleton shirt and khaki pants with razor-sharp creases. It was the standard look for boys from East L.A. circa 1959.

Alex was a year ahead of me in elementary school. I was a close friend of his cousin Connie. Connie's family and Alex's lived in the nearby "projects." Many of the students at our school were first generation Mexican-Americans. They had one foot in their parents' mariachi and ranchero music and the other in rock and roll.

I was one of only a handful of Caucasian students at my school. My parents had purchased a new tract home in the Monterey Hills above East L.A. Junior College on the G.I. Bill. The culture I encountered there was completely different from the middle-class, Jewish culture I had grown up with in West L.A. Living in East L.A. was like visiting an exotic foreign country, full of vibrant Mexican music, spicy cooking smells, and the lovely cadence of the Spanish language.

One day Connie asked me if I "liked" Alex. I didn't know him, but I guessed he had seen me and asked his cousin to intervene. She invited me to her house to meet him. Nervous and excited, I wore my tightest cut-off jeans and a yellow and white crop top with just a hint of midriff showing. I remember slow dancing with Alex in Connie's living room to a smoldering oldie, "Smoke Gets in Your Eyes" by The Platters.

As we swayed together to the romantic song, I inhaled the floral perfume of his pomade. His brown cheek was as soft as velvet next to mine. By the time the dance ended, our hands were sticky with sweat. I remember feeling somewhat embarrassed but happy. He looked as though he felt the same way.

A few days later my phone rang. "Hello," I answered.

"This is Alex." Pause.

"Oh, hi." Pause.

"Uh, would you like to go around with me?" Major pause.

"Um, I don't think my parents will let me."

"Oh . . . O.K. Bye."

Shaky with excitement, I hung up the phone. Alex had just asked me to go steady with him, but I knew I was too young to have a boyfriend. I was 11.

I didn't encounter him again until the next semester when I began 7th grade. One day I saw him in the hall and said hello, grinning. He just looked past me as though I didn't exist. Shocked, confused, and embarrassed by his snub, I felt my face redden as I fought back tears. I quickly walked out of the building.

Shortly after that, my social studies teacher Mr. Rosen met my parents at back-to-school night. "I think it would be in Myra's best interest if you took her out of Griffith Junior High and placed her in a more challenging school, especially if you want her to attend college," he advised them. That summer my parents sold our house and moved back to West L.A. where my new junior high was one of the best in the county.

I never lost the legacy of my pre-teen years in East L.A. Salsa and mariachi music, the rich smell of enchiladas and carnitas, certain slang phrases in Spanish—they all quicken my heartbeat still. And I never forgot the scent of Alex's pomade.

*Here I am at age 11*

# Beside the Seaside

*By Linda Zirk*

When Easter 1953 rolled around, my family gathered at Nana Polly's house for the annual discussion of our two-week summer holiday. The grown-ups pored over *Dalton's Weekly*, a guide to real estate for purchase and for rent, to see what holiday lets were available.

"Here's one for Littlehampton," exclaimed Auntie Joan. "Close to the beach—easy access to the prom and fun fair."

"Yes, but can we get four separate bungalows in the same area?" asked my dad.

"What about going to Hayling Island this year? We've never been down to Hampshire before," offered Uncle Nobby.

Soon everyone placed special requests:

"Essex has nice sandy beaches."

"Not so easy to get to, though, since we'd have to go through London."

"What about Cornwall or Devon? Oh, think of the real clotted cream with scones we could get down there!"

Post-WW II Britain was full of ration books, housing and utility shortages. Life could be very dreary. The one event everyone looked forward to was the family summer holiday in August. School holidays started the last week of July and ended the first week of September. So families crammed as much as they could into those precious six weeks. How we longed for hot summer days at the beach!

Nana Polly had been wheelchair-bound due to rheumatoid arthritis for about six years by this time, so the family arranged the holiday around her needs. Easy access to holiday bungalows and caravans was a

14

*Adventures*

key issue. We also needed to be close to the beach, and a nice promenade was an added attraction. That's where the local cafes and tea shops were located. A fun fair with a Ferris wheel, a roller coaster, and arcade games would be the icing on the cake.

Besides Nana, our group included Uncle Jim and Auntie Pat and their twins; Auntie Cath and Uncle Marc and their two sons; Uncle Nobby and Auntie Joan and their daughter Janice, as well as Mum, Dad, Susan and me. Other assorted second cousins and great aunts and uncles often joined the fun. We children were very much the same age, with Susan the oldest and Janice the youngest. In fact, four of us were born within eight weeks of each other in 1947.

The kids in the family never really knew exactly where we were going or where we would stay. It might be on a farm or in a small village, perhaps in a caravan or maybe a bungalow. But we were always in walking distance of the beach, so we could take our buckets and spades and swimsuits and buy sticky rock candy to eat.

My dad was the only car owner in the family, so it fell to Mum and Dad to transport Nana, the wheelchair, and some of the luggage to our destination. One of the uncles also traveled by car to help Mum and Dad, but the rest of the family, sometimes numbering 12-15 people, arrived via train or coach. My sister Susan was usually the designated child who rode along in the car, but for me the journey with my uncles and aunties and cousins was an additional treat. Riding in the coach, which carried other holiday makers to the same seaside town, was the best way. Everyone shared sandwiches and tips on what to do when we arrived. Children of all ages sat together at the back of the coach and told stories of past adventures.

English beaches are not always sandy. Often they can be quite stony, so it was difficult to push and secure Nana's wheelchair to a safe location while the family frolicked on the beach. Uncle Nobby carried Nana while others secured her wheelchair, so she had a good view of all of us. With her tartan rug over her lap, and a sun umbrella attached to the handles of the wheelchair, she designated our location on the busy beach.

Everyone helped to carry our daily picnic basket, umbrellas, and towels to the beach, with the kids responsible for their own buckets and spades and other sandcastle-building paraphernalia. Woe betide us if, during the day, we lost anything!

"Where's my bucket and spade?" one of the cousins wailed.

"Can we play beach cricket?" the boys asked.

"Who wants to be the first one in the sea?" Auntie Joan inquired. Auntie Joan was a good swimmer, so she was responsible for making sure the kids were safe in the surf. All of us children were introduced to swimming in the cold English Channel water.

We loved it best when we were on a sandy beach because that meant sandcastles, beach cricket, and races against the grown-ups. The morning flew by, and soon Mum called everyone back to Nana's chair for lunch of sandwiches and apples. What would it be today—cheese and pickle? ham and tomato? strawberry jam? And of course sand in the sandwiches.

Around lunchtime, the uncles took a walk along the prom. As a child, I never fully understood why they didn't want sand-laden sandwiches. As I grew older, I realized there was a pub on the promenade where they would relax over a pint of beer and a pub sandwich. The best part about their walk was the bags of crisps they brought back to us for an afternoon snack.

By four o'clock in the afternoon, it was time for tea, so we packed up and trekked back to the prom in search of a café for a nice hot cuppa and a tea cake. As we walked through the fun fair, the smells of sugary cotton candy and fresh popcorn with melted butter beckoned.

At the arcade, the uncles showed the boys how to shoot a rifle at metal cowboy hats—pop-pop-pop! The shrieks of the riders on the Big Dipper and the Waltzer reminded me how I longed to get older and bigger, so I could ride the Ferris wheel and roller coasters. I was still stuck riding a small merry-go-round.

At day's end we faced a long walk home, kids cranky and tired. Janice, the youngest, found a place on Nana's lap for the ride. To keep up our spirits, someone started singing:

*Oh, I do like to be beside the seaside,*

*I do like to be beside the sea.*

*Oh, I do like to walk along the prom, prom, prom,*

*Where the brass band plays tiddley-pom-pom-pom.*

Soon campfire songs, rounds, and old familiar music hall ballads filled the air. The chorus of familiar voices made even the long walk back to our bungalow part of the seaside magic.

*Sussex Beach*

# Dakota Days

*By Liz Helgerson*

I always think of October as the "most likely to be glorious" month in South Dakota. The days are often cool but sun kissed; the trees show off their fall coats, red and yellow; and summer clouds of mosquitos and gnats have been banished by early night-time frosts. Year after year, Mother Nature at her best plays hostess at the University of South Dakota's homecoming event, Dakota Days.

As a young child, I was enchanted by the brightly decorated fraternity and sorority houses whose displays depicted hometown team-mascot Coyotes triumphing over their gridiron opposition. On Friday night, my family walked the town to admire the displays. I wondered at such engineering marvels as papier-mâché footballs that flew into the arms of jubilant Coyotes. I yearned to grow up enough to become more than a spectator, to be transformed into one of the sophisticated and beautiful college girls who filled the streets and sidewalks.

On Saturday morning, USD's homecoming parade provided the entertainment. I loved it all: the blast of music from approaching bands; the bands' front rows of beautiful baton-twirling girls; the sometimes clever and always colorful floats which bore yet more triumphant Coyotes, and still more pretty prom-dress-clad girls; even the convertibles filled with dignitaries who waved in passing to the cheering bystanders. And, as if more excitement were needed, the float riders often threw fistfuls of candy which we kids dived into the street to collect, not wanting to be outdone by our neighbors.

Saturday afternoon, however, brought the best part of my childhood Dakota Days. It was the time when many of the adults and virtually all of the college students went off to the game. The town was small, and wherever we children went, we could hear the bands and drums echoing in the stadium. We knew by the loud cheering whenever the Coyotes made a touchdown. Even we ticketless children felt the drama of the big game although we were highly distracted by our own important business.

Since the parade festivities were over, and only the winning floats were welcome at the football field, the non-winning entries were fair game. They sat abandoned beside the fraternity and sorority houses, waiting to be dismantled after the planned homecoming parties. So, with the tacit approval of the float builders (and our parents, of course), the children of Vermillion were allowed to start the demolition. Imagine the glorious streamers, tassels, fringes and pompoms we gleaned from those floats. What fun we had as we competed to decorate the most sparkly and eye-catching bike! We wove streamers through the spokes of the wheels, hung fringe around the baskets, and suspended pompoms from the handlebars. For more than a week after, if the fall rains held off, we held our own parades on the way to school.

By the time I was in high school, Dakota Days felt quite different. The fraternity house decorations looked a little amateurish and unoriginal to me. After all, I'd already seen plenty of triumphant Coyotes before. I still toured the town's decorations, of course, but now with jaded eyes, with friends not family, and with more interest in impressing those friends than in viewing the displays. Somehow, the college girls didn't seem so princess-like any more, their beauty not so far out of reach. Nor was there any sense in helping to dismantle the floats. I wouldn't be caught dead riding a bike—and certainly wouldn't call attention to it with a bunch of tacky decorations.

As for the parade, I was now in it—a clarinet-blowing member of the Marching Tanagers. Truth be told, marching didn't really suit me. We band members wore old uniforms that looked like ill-fitting men's suits, right down to the white dress shirts and Windsor ties. I admit to envying my more popular classmates who marched in front as drum majorette, baton twirlers and cheerleaders. With their cute costumes and short skirts, they were the ones stealing admiring looks as our band passed by.

I envied them, that is, until October 1962, when it froze and snowed on Dakota Day. Under my stupid old uniform, I could wear long-johns.

With the tips cut off an old pair of gloves, I could play clarinet with minimal frost bite. At the end of the parade, I actually felt sorry for my cheerleader sister and the rest of the front-line girls, whose legs had turned blue and hands had stiffened around pompoms and batons. That day I found an upside to being who I was – the awkward little sister of the high school prom queen, no doubt, but still a person smart enough to wear warm clothes on a cold and icy day.

Whenever I experienced Dakota Days as an adult, I found myself a mere spectator again, a real outsider even when I attended as a member of the university staff. Those homecoming Saturdays brought crisp and warm weather. The maple trees glowed in the bright fall sunshine. University faculty, students, old couples, and families with young children crowded along the parade route as in earlier years. But, as the parade passed by, the participants seemed incredibly young to my eyes, the floats barely decorated. They carried no clever scenes animated by fearsome Coyotes as I expected. Instead, they bore groups of young people (cute boys and darling girls, certainly) who had been chosen to represent their fraternities, sororities or other clubs. Among them I noted quite a few students from my classes, some of whom were clearly inebriated. I did not attend the afternoon football game, and while I could still hear the bands and cheering crowds in the stadium, I felt neither the thrill of victory nor the disappointment of defeat.

I attended Dakota Days for the last time in 1992. By then, I had little attachment to the university, nor to the celebration itself. Instead, the event served as a convenient excuse to take a long weekend from work and from my strained marital relationship. It meant I could visit my mother, who still lived in town, see a few old friends who were making the homecoming trip, and take stock of my life. In retrospect, I think I mostly wanted to get back in touch with the person I used to be.

That year Mother Nature outdid herself again, regaling Dakota Day visitors with a bright fall day, just cool enough to require a light jacket. I enjoyed wandering through the crowd of parade goers, eager to join my best grade-school friend on our traditional corner along the route. We reminisced, applauded the bands, and gave high-fives to the children who caught candies as floats passed by. Our loudest cheers, however, were reserved for a passing convertible that held a special dignitary, high-school colleague Tim Johnson, who was then serving as the junior U.S. Senator of South Dakota.

It was, in sum, a glorious day. It made me nostalgic to stand there. No longer enchanted, no longer yearning and envious, I still felt the allure —though I'm not sure of what—perhaps the innocence of those brightly decorated bikes.

*Awaiting the parade in 1992 with Barb Sterling and Barb Remington*

# Grandma's House

By Marilyn Hamilton

The wide tree-lined avenue in Pasadena called Paloma Street is the street my grandma lives on. My sister and I are going to spend the weekend with Grandma and Grandpa. I am seven and Judie is five. I love this street with its sidewalks and old homes. All the houses are different: some English Tudor like my grandma's, some Spanish style, and some are California bungalows. We arrive at 1880 Paloma, and Judie and I take our small suitcase inside to the front bedroom.

We always sleep together in the big bed in the front room because Grandma and Grandpa have the back bedroom with twin beds. When my cousin David comes, we all pile in and sleep in the big bed together. Grandma, a large woman with flesh hanging from her arms, is the best cook. Grandpa is tall and slender and has a voice designed to put everyone to sleep. He regales the family with stories, and I am not the only one dozing off.

I sigh with pleasure. A weekend filled with reading my Nancy Drew book and the National Geographic magazines in the warm sunroom on the side of the house or exploring the old armoire in the basement with its colorful robes and an assortment of other objects to dress up in. I especially like donning the red Chinese silk robe.

My favorite activity, however, is to roller skate around the block. I have metal skates that I strap onto my shoes. The skates have a metal key for tightening the fit. I push off with my right leg, then my left leg, and I'm off for a long skate. Grandma's house is in the middle of a long block, and I go right to Allen Street. On the corner is a small bungalow, and I stop to talk with the lady who lives there. Down to the stoplight at Orange Grove. I could skate on Orange Grove all day and look at the large lovely homes, each different. Some are two stories, and I like to imagine living in a house where I can be upstairs looking out the window at the birds flying and the treetops waving.

I arrive at the home behind Grandma and Grandpa's, and I knock on the door. I visit with the woman who lives there, and she shows me the harp her daughter plays. It is such a lovely instrument with so many strings. She plucks a few so I can hear how it sounds. Time to continue skating. I come to the corner of Elm where I turn toward Paloma Street. One more stop to see if the twins are visiting their grandparents at the house on Elm and Paloma. No, they aren't there this weekend. Too bad— no other kids for Judie and me to play with this time.

Off I skate on the smooth sidewalk, so much better than at home where the pavement is uneven and rough. I still have a big scab on my knee where I fell last week. I always seem to have a scab on my knee or elbow, but that's the price I pay to be outside having fun. Home now

to Grandma's house. I will go inside and have some lemonade in the sunny breakfast nook overlooking the backyard bougainvillea.

The weekend at Grandma's is special because she doesn't make us do chores, and she spoils us with good things to eat and fun things to do. It is our retreat. Grandma's house is simply the best.

*With my younger sister Judie in 1949*

*Adventures*

# On the Set in Utah

*By Myra Lathrop*

The dry desert air burned our eyes and parched our throats, but there was something exciting about being on the road in a place so alien to us. Miles of straight blacktop and sand stretched endlessly ahead with no trees in sight.

School was out for summer vacation. My nine-year-old self was excited beyond expression because my mom, five-year-old brother Joel, and I were driving from L.A. to Kanab, Utah, to spend several weeks with my dad on location. He was the head make-up artist on a western TV series entitled "Boots & Saddles." The story line followed the Fifth Cavalry in the Arizona territories of the 1880s, as they tried to co-exist with the Apache.

"What's it going to be like, Mom?" I whined several times. She had packed bathing suits; I knew that was a good sign. Soon our suitcases, a hamper full of food, and a huge jug of cold lemonade were stowed in our blue and white '56 Chevy Bel Air. With no air-conditioning, we rolled down the car windows as we headed northeast of L.A. into the desert. Our destination was Las Vegas for an overnight stay, a break in the 478-mile trip.

Mom later admitted that this was one of the most daring things she had ever done. I remember dropping ice cubes down the back of her blouse to help keep her cool as she drove through the summer heat. About ten miles outside of Vegas, as dusk began to envelop us, our car developed vapor lock. Mom, looking hot, tired, and hungry, hailed a passing truck driver who took us the rest of the way into town where she called a tow truck.

*Adventures*

We checked into a motel where we promptly changed into swimsuits and soaked in the cold pool before going to bed. Mom said not to wake her early the next morning. She left some bills on the table, so we could have pancakes at the attached diner. Car fixed and bodies refreshed, we were off to Utah before noon.

By the time we reached Kanab, the scenery had changed to red rock country full of cottonwood trees. The sky was the bluest blue I had ever seen. At the center of this postage-stamp town was Parry Lodge, our home for the next two weeks. It seemed like a magic kingdom with its huge swimming pool and attached restaurant where we could order whatever our hearts desired. Best of all were the butterscotch sundaes after dinner: ice cold vanilla ice cream topped with warm sticky sauce and whipped cream. I was sure it couldn't get any better.

But it did. Each day we went out to the "fort" where the series was filmed. My dad had been putting make-up on cowboys and Indians since 4:00 a.m. I was shocked to see that the Indians were really white actors covered in dark body make-up, donning black wigs with braids.

My brother and I watched in awe as the Indians and cavalry fought to the death on their beautiful horses. Stuntmen dropped from high atop the fort towers, pierced by arrows, and Indians were shot off their steeds. We were amazed by the batches of blood Dad had to mix and smear on these actors. Lunchtime found us in line with the whole crew, piling our plates with barbecued meats, baked beans and cold potato salad. After lunch we drove back to the lodge and swam for a while; later, we crossed the practically empty road to Foster Freeze for ice cream cones.

After we returned home, we were thrilled to see our dad's name listed as make-up artist whenever we watched "Boots and Saddles" on our black-and-white TV. I wasted no time informing my friends that the so-called Indians had on body make-up, and the blood was fake, created by my dad in our kitchen sink. I felt proud and important to be the daughter of a Hollywood make-up artist.

In 2004, and again in 2019, I passed through Kanab on the way to Zion and Bryce national parks. It was still a tiny town. Parry Lodge was there, just as I remembered it, painted white and surrounded by trees.

When I walked inside, I saw scores of photos on the walls depicting films that had been shot in the area over the decades.

Gazing at the photos of cowboys and Indians, I realized just how special that trip to Kanab was; it was the first time and the only time I watched my dad ply his trade as a professional make-up artist.

Parry Lodge, Kanab Utah,
62 years later

# First Girls:
# The Adventure Begins

*By Linda Zirk*

In 1972, at 25 years old, I was in the doldrums. England was again experiencing union strikes, especially in the coal mines, causing utility shortages. My cousins and friends were all marrying and having babies. I was the odd one out—no steady boyfriend, and no real wish to get married just because everyone else was doing it.

I was reading a copy of *The Lady* magazine someone had left behind on the morning train when I saw a job opening that sounded intriguing. FIRST GIRL, an American placement agency, was advertising for professional secretaries to work in New York and Chicago. With feminism in full swing, American women had abandoned the secretarial field for positions with more responsibility. According to FIRST GIRL, British, Irish and Australian secretaries were considered the best in the world.

The position promised a guaranteed salary (twice as much as I was then making in London), a Social Security card, an alien registration card, plus a round-trip airline ticket and accommodation in a women's residential apartment building. It all seemed too good to be true. The only caveat was that we had to agree to work for the agency for a period of six months. I applied and within six months I was ready to depart.

On January 11, 1973, I was at Heathrow Airport with my parents—who were sure I was being sold into some form of slavery. I noticed two other girls standing with their parents carrying the same large envelope I had been given. This envelope contained chest x-rays and other medical information we needed to provide to U.S. Immigration when we arrived at Kennedy Airport.

We were all excited to find each other in the crowd of people milling around passport control. Jackie was 20; she had a thick northern accent and spoke fast, so it was difficult to understand her. She wore a brown leather mini-skirt and short-sleeved, low-necked blouse and had a leather jacket over her arm. Mary was a 19-year-old southeast England girl— very pretty, with long flowing blond hair, dressed in yellow linen trousers and a white sweater. Later we learned she was fleeing the U.K. because she was convinced she could become a model in the U.S. I was wearing a black wool maxi-skirt with a lavender silk shirt, black knee-high boots, and carried a fur hat. This was, after all, January, and we were going to New York City. I thought I was very stylish.

The three of us made our way to the BOAC boarding area and finalized our seat assignments. Our final FIRST GIRL seat mate, Sarah, was one of the last to board the plane. She got lost after she went through passport control. Sarah was 21 and very unsure of herself. She wore a sensible knee-length skirt and a twin-set. As soon as we were seated, the conversations started. Jackie was extremely garrulous and laughingly said, "So are you leaving a boyfriend behind? I am, because me mam and dad don't think he's good enough for me. But I'm not sad about it, 'cos I know he'll wait for six months." The rest of us weren't leaving any boyfriends behind.

"I hope I get a job in advertising with *Vogue* or one of the other magazines. I'd really like to have some professional photographs taken," Mary offered.

Shy Sarah introduced herself saying, "I worked at the BBC, and think Tony Blackburn (the morning DJ on Radio 1) is absolutely fabulous. My friend Heather is his personal assistant."

Four or five years older than the other girls, I was more interested in finding out if they were adventurous enough to travel to other parts of the U.S. "So have you all traveled outside of England before?" I asked.

"Not really," replied Jackie. "Although me, my mam and dad went on a camping holiday to Wales one year. I was about 9, and it poured rain all the time we were in the tent."

Lunch was served, and the first disaster struck. Mary spilled her coffee all over her yellow trousers. We helped her mop up, and she slid out of the trousers as the rest of us shielded her from fellow passengers. Mary rang the call button and explained what had happened to the attendant. She asked if she could get her suitcase so she could change. The attendant explained that the luggage was in the hold below us. Nothing could be retrieved until we landed. Tears rolled down Mary's face.

I had two coats in my carry-on luggage, so I told Mary she could wear my raincoat when we exited the plane. In the meantime we fashioned a skirt out of one of the blankets. It was beginning to look as if I was going to become a mother hen to these chicks.

After we landed at Kennedy Airport, I suggested that the four of us wait until everyone else had deplaned, so that we could help Mary with her newly-rigged skirt. We still needed to go through passport control and immigration. We had been given instructions by the FIRST GIRL London office about what to expect and what documents to have ready.

I was first in line at the immigration booth (not the usual passport control) and told the officer that the four of us were together in the same program. That seemed to ease the way for everyone. He kindly called the other girls over in order to process us altogether. Then disaster #2 struck. Sarah had left her big envelope on the plane. In tears, she started to backtrack toward the plane, only to be told by the immigration officer, "I'm sorry, Ma'am. You can't go back out that door. You're in no-man's land until we see all the paperwork." Uh-oh, I thought. We'll never get out of here, and Bill Meacham, the agency owner, is waiting for us. It turned out, however, that immigration really didn't need to see the medical envelope. Disaster averted.

Feeling a little more confident, we left immigration and headed for our luggage. When we entered the arrivals hall, we found Bill smiling and holding a welcome sign. At his side was another young woman. An Australian, Jillian was 21 and had spent the Christmas and New Year's holidays in Iowa with friends from the exchange student program she had attended.

Once we were all comfortably seated in Bill's enormous station wagon, we started jabbering away, trying to understand Jillian's Aussie slang and Jackie's thick Lancashire accent, asking Bill a million questions about the sights we along the way. Finally we reached our destination, the Webster Apartments at 419 W. 34th Street.

We were given our keys and told to settle in. Dinner would be available from 6–8 p.m. Since this was a female-only residence apartment building, Bill couldn't join us for dinner, but he suggested that we all meet at 6 p.m. in the parlor and go down to dinner together.

The rest of the evening passed in a blur. We met many other First Girls, some of whom were eating dinner before going out for the evening. All I wanted to do was take a nice long nap, but somehow Jillian and I stayed up late chatting about our families, our travels, our hopes for the future.

As the weeks passed, life settled down, but the one constant was Thursday dinner at the Webster Apartments. That was the day that new First Girls arrived, mostly one or two at a time. Mary quickly moved out. No one was really sure where she went. Jackie and I discovered our mutual love of dancing, and off we'd go to a club on Friday evenings.

Two new arrivals came a couple of weeks later, Pam and Jessica. And then shortly after that Diana and Jane arrived, followed by Laura and Carole. I'm sure there were other lovely First Girls who arrived during 1973, but these new arrivals took weekend trips with Jillian and me, traveling up and down the East Coast, exploring American history in Boston, New York, Washington, D.C., and Philadelphia, and taking a side trip to Niagara Falls.

By this time Jillian had become my First Friend in New York—and to this day we are in constant contact even though we are separated by more than 3,000 miles. We attended each other's weddings, and she is my daughter's godmother. We stay with her whenever we visit the New York area, and we toured Australia with her. I have lost contact with Jackie, but Sarah and I remain friends and meet whenever we can. She now lives in Brisbane, Australia, so London is our only convenient meeting place.

Pam, Jessica, Laura, Carole, Jane, and Diana flew in from England; Sarah flew in from Australia; I flew in in from California, and together with Jillian we celebrated our fortieth FIRST GIRL anniversary — and yes, we stayed at the Webster Apartments in New York City. I couldn't have imagined in 1973 that taking a position with FIRST GIRL would introduce me to a wonderful new group of lifelong friends, as well as a new country.

*Celebrating our 40th FIRST GIRL anniversary in New York City*

# My New Front Teeth

*By Shirley Summers*

Going to the dentist has always produced anxiety for me. I never allowed my children to see me in the dental chair because it would have affected their entire dental experience. For them, a trip to the dentist meant that you got a new toy and a new toothbrush. For me, it means that I cannot anticipate when I will experience pain; even the noise of the drill makes me feel that pain is imminent.

As soon as I sit in the dental chair, my hands grip the arms of the chair; my knuckles turn white, and my entire body is tense. If the dentist makes a move I did not anticipate, I have been known to jump. I have tried meditation, making small talk, and other relaxation techniques, but as hard as I try, I do not relax until I am ready to go home.

So I was not thrilled when my dentist first approached me about having crowns made for my front teeth. "I doubt that your insurance will pay for it, as there is no medical basis for the procedure," he said. "It is purely for aesthetic reasons."

My first thought was that he might be trying to line his pocketbook. I asked him the price, and when he told me, I was aghast. My teeth have always been healthy; I haven't had cavities for a long time. I spend my discretionary money on travel or something else I want to do, not on a choice someone else has made for me. I asked the dentist to submit a request to the insurance company for an estimate.

As I thought about whether or not to have the work done, I began to notice people with beautiful shiny white teeth and younger smiles. It was nothing dramatic, but it was noticeable. I wondered whether all of these people had the same procedure done that I was considering. Friends began to tell me that they were getting elective dental work done. One said that after the work was completed, her teeth felt big. Another friend said she had dental work done to improve her appearance.

When the estimate came back from my insurance company, they were willing to pay 80% of the cost. That would leave me with $2,000 left to pay. The willingness of my insurance company to invest $8,000 and the input I received from friends were pushing me toward having the work done. I even consulted actuarial tables based upon my age and health. The tables revealed I have a long time to live, so I made the appointment.

As I was driving to the dentist's office, I began to think about all of the things that I could spend $2,000 on, rather than my teeth. When I arrived, there was no one waiting, so I had no chance to change my mind. After I sat in the dental chair, the dental assistant reclined the seat, and the smiling dentist came into the room. Immediately I thought about the long needle coming. Just relax, I told myself.

As we waited for the medication to numb my mouth, the dentist asked if I had taken any trips lately. But with the medication beginning to work, I was definitely not articulate. He talked about some TED talks that he had recently listened to and a hike he would take soon. After a while, my mouth was completely numb. I closed my eyes as they began to work.

Before long, water sprayed all over my face and down my neck. I wanted to grab a Kleenex or a towel to wipe it away, but I was afraid of breaking their concentration. And the sound of the awful drill kept me anxious. They were confident about this procedure. I was the only one who was new to it.

As they continued working on my teeth, drilling and spraying water, I began to notice that the air was light, and I was actually beginning to relax. My hands no longer gripped the arms of the chair; they actually rested in my lap. Now it was time for impressions to be taken. I revisited my adolescence when I had impressions done before I got braces. Those impressions made me gag.

Fortunately, impressions have changed over the last 50 years. I did not gag, and I did not throw up. I wanted to say something, but with a blue-gloved hand in front of my face and a blue finger in my mouth to hold the impression tray in place, I was prevented from saying anything at all. I decided to save my comments for later, but then forgot what I had planned to say. I had been sitting in the dental chair for three hours. My smart watch kept telling me it was time to stand up. My body told me it was time to go to the bathroom.

In the bathroom, I could not resist the urge to look in the mirror. My six front teeth looked like spindles of teeth that had worn away due to lack of care. I looked like an old woman who had no dental insurance and no financial means, someone who lived in severe poverty. When I returned to my chair, the dentist said, "You didn't look in the mirror or take any pictures, did you?"

"I looked in the mirror to see the process," I replied. "But I did not take any pictures." This stage of the process was not going to be recorded for history.

At the end of four hours, my dental experience was completed, and I could hardly talk. My mouth was numb, and my nose felt huge, but when I looked in the mirror, I felt a sense of satisfaction. Instead of my coffee-stained 76-year-old teeth, I could join my friends with younger-looking teeth.

*My new front teeth*

Six months after I had crowns put on my upper six teeth, I look in the mirror, and I am pleased. My front teeth are even, and all are the same color. I now realize how badly stained my teeth were from drinking coffee. Fifty-five years is a long time to be drinking coffee on a daily basis. When I look at my new teeth, my smile seems brighter. I feel younger, more confident, and more ready to face the challenges that lie ahead.

# Challenges

"The change that we dread the most may
become our salvation."

*Barbara Kingsolver*

# A Capitol Fourth

*By Liz Helgerson*

How could I possibly be here now? I pinched myself as the light faded and a crescent moon showed itself over the Washington Monument.

I hadn't expected anything like this when I made the decision to start a new life in the nation's capital. I probably would not have had the courage to move had my dear childhood friend, Barbara Remington, not lived in the D.C. suburbs. She welcomed me like a long-lost cousin – helped me find and furnish an apartment and included me in gatherings with other old South Dakota friends. Among those were three people essential to this special moment, Ron Helgerson, and Tim and Barbara Johnson.

Ron had been widowed three years previously. His late wife was a dear college friend of the Johnsons and the younger sister of a boy I dated in high school. Tim, who had graduated from Vermillion High the year after me, was currently serving as the Junior Senator of South Dakota. In the three years since my arrival in Washington, we had all socialized occasionally.

It was 1997, and Ron and I had quite recently become an item, despite the fact that he was living in Los Angeles—all the way across the country. How pleased I was when he planned his summer vacation to include a four-day visit in Washington over Independence Day. The only complication: his high-school-aged son Gus, who adamantly opposed our relationship. Knowing how difficult it would be to please Gus, Ron had arranged for him to stay with Tim and Barbara, who had a daughter the same age, while he stayed with me.

The days were tense, as Ron, Gus and I toured D.C. together. Gus refused to walk with us, trailing as sullenly as he could some 20 feet behind as we visited the Mall and its Smithsonian museums. "Dad," he would occasionally call out, "I want to talk with you." His father was forced to leave me to walk alone through the museums.

"I'm so sorry," Ron said to me repeatedly.

"Don't worry, I'm O.K." I replied. And it was true. Indeed, I felt for Gus, recognizing his sorrow and his fear and anger at his dad for "replacing" his mother. But, truth be told, I was already so much in love, it did not matter that Gus was making the days unpleasant.

For the evening of the 4th, we all planned to meet at the bleachers below the Capitol building to share a potluck picnic and see the fireworks. "There will be a crowd," Barbara Johnson warned. "We will meet at the back entrance to the Capitol. You know where that is?"

"Sure," Ron replied. "We'll see you there. I'll bring the dessert. I'm thinking cherry hand pies will fit the day."

Ron and I took the subway downtown in the late afternoon, amazed by the number of people who could cram into the cars. We mounted the escalator in front of the Smithsonian Castle, and our crowd spewed like a flooding river onto the flat open spaces of the Washington Mall. That day, however, the space wasn't open. It was filled with a crowd of more than 600,000 visitors, according to later estimates.

An International Folk Festival was underway, entertaining the late afternoon crowds with tents full of representative folk art. Buskers sporting bright regional costumes performed gymnastic tricks. Food trucks offered exotic treats. We wandered from tent to tent and music venue to music venue. The U.S. was represented by a Jewish klezmer jazz band, which did an incredible job of melding the black African rhythms and melodies of New Orleans with New York City's klezmer instrumentation of accordion, clarinet and violin.

Nearby, a group from Lithuania countered the high spirits of the klezmer band with mournful dirges, underscored by the morenka, their regional variant on a bagpipe. The band's morenka player demonstrated how he could simultaneously breathe in and out, producing the constant, monotone droning that characterized their music. The new experiences made everything sparkle, despite the damp heat of a Washington summer day. We wandered happily through the crowds, relishing the exotic atmosphere almost as much as each other's company.

When the time came to join Gus and our friends, we headed for the designated meeting place. Alas, the Capitol's back entrance was nowhere to be found. In vain, we circled the building, spotting neither the entryway nor any of our friends. As we searched, the crowds continued to converge on Capitol Hill, staking out places for viewing the fireworks. The bleachers were already completely full.

We didn't quite panic. We knew we could get home, after all, and we could connect with everyone later. But, we had the dessert. And Gus would feel even more abandoned if we didn't manage to find him.

Suddenly, Barb Remington's daughter appeared at our side. She had decided to play scout and miraculously picked us out of the crowd. "Follow me," she said. "And don't get lost again!" Surprise followed surprise as she led us to a door, spoke briefly to the guard, and ushered us into the interior of the Capitol. Along a dark hallway and up the stairs we went, suddenly emerging on the Capitol balcony. Our whole gang was there; only one other small group had staked out a spot nearby. It was as if we had been elevated above the common people in the crowds below.

Barb Johnson explained the change in plans. "By the time we had waited for you, it was impossible to get our group onto the bleachers," she said. "People were pushing and shoving. There was no room for us, even without the cooler. Tim decided there was nothing to do but to pull rank. He talked to the guards, and convinced them that, as a Senator, he had a perfect right to entertain his little group on the balcony. So, here we are!"

Indeed, there we were. The evening's magic opened the door to a future like none I had ever imagined. I knew then that I would follow my heart wherever Ron would take it. I did not know, however, how many years would go by before Gus accepted me; how many ways he would find to show his displeasure; and how warm a relationship we would build and enjoy today.

*Challenges*

As we finished our hand pies, the National Orchestra began to play. My heart strained with the fullness of it all—old friends, new love, skyrockets in flight.

*Fireworks over the Capitol*

# Internet Dating at 70

*By Myra Lathrop*

Click! I hit the button that sends my photo through cyberspace and attaches it to my written profile on Match.com. I'm sure I have not taken a deep breath in at least ten minutes, and my shoulders are tight. What have I done? It's too late for second or third thoughts; after stressing over this for weeks, I have done the deed.

Friends encouraged me to give internet dating a try. They all know someone who knows someone else who met a true love on one of the dating services, usually Match. And like so many other women my age, my response was "never."

Despite my full, varied life—volunteering, participating in interest groups, and socializing with a circle of smart, stimulating friends— I sometimes felt lonely when I became a widow. I especially noticed my isolation on weekends when married pals typically spend time with their spouses.

Living in a small, fairly conservative town doesn't help. I don't belong to a church or any civic organizations, and I am far too old to put on skin-tight flashy leggings with 3-inch stilettos and march off to a local bar. What's a 70-year-old woman who is still alive and kicking to do?

I agonized over writing my profile. I took meticulous care to describe myself physically and mentally. I mentioned my interests, my core values, and my goals for a relationship. I made it clear that companionship and affection are primary. I also emphasized that I am not interested in living with someone or marrying again.

My three-month subscription on Match entitled me to see photos and read descriptions of men in my area who met my qualifications and shared my interests. I listed an age range of 63–75 and said I wasn't interested in anyone who lived more than fifty miles away.

One of the disconcerting aspects of Match, I discovered, is that women are encouraged to message men whose profiles or photos they find enticing. Having grown up in an era when that was not the dating protocol, I found this daunting. I have been married three times and dated in between these relationships, but I never made the first move. Although I consider myself a feminist, I couldn't cross that line. But a woman of 70 might have to push beyond her comfort zone to nudge a man to respond.

In addition, I needed to check the site at least once a day to see whether anyone had "viewed" me, or perhaps even signaled that he "liked" me—a Match term denoting interest. If there was a highlighted "like," the algorithm began an email for me. But if this person "liked" me, why didn't he send me an email?

The website also chooses daily matches, again using their proprietary algorithm. At the top of each photo is a percentage which supposedly represents interests we share.

As I expected, I didn't receive too many responses initially. Most men around my age are looking for younger, sometimes much younger women. Really? Didn't they have a friend check the photo they submitted? So many full-bearded, scruffy-looking, unsmiling men in their 60s and 70s. And with few exceptions, their profiles were laughable.

*Sixty-five year old retired contractor looking for women 45–55, slender, sexy, into sports and watching TV. Must love dogs. I have three. Two grown children who live at home off and on. I enjoy riding my motorcycle on weekends, watching football and baseball, and going to country western concerts. I like to go camping in my small but comfortable camper. It would be more fun with you!*

My profile detailed my interests in music, dance, literature, film, theatre, nature walks, and fine dining. In addition, I made a special point of saying exercise and good health are important to me. I emphasized that I was an atheist and liberal. Can you guess how often a man who described himself as a conservative Christian responded to my profile? If you guessed half of my responders, you would be right. So much for the accuracy of Match's algorithm. I also received replies from men who live in Las Vegas, San Francisco, L.A., and Fresno. Either these guys don't read, or they didn't care about what I had written. Probably both. I must say I had many good laughs as I read the profiles of men considered potential matches.

When a man who lived in my area "liked" me, I read his scanty profile. He was friendly, so I decided to jump in and practice the meeting scenario at a local coffee shop. He looked like his photo: so far, so good. We walked across the street to the park and began to chat. He was quite amiable, and he had a nice smile.

His profile had been non-committal about his political beliefs. In relating some of his childhood, he actually made an overtly racist remark. I was too shocked to respond when he declared that Trump was doing a good job, especially for the white people in our country. "I really don't think we are a match," I replied. "Did you actually read my profile?"

"Yeah."

"I need to get home now," I replied. He smiled as we walked back to the coffee shop where our cars were parked.

"Would you like to go to the coast for lunch next Saturday?" he asked.

I opened my car door, and blurted, "It won't work. Good luck to you." He was still smiling as I drove away.

Another man I met had recently retired from his chiropractic practice. He was well-educated, liberal, in great shape, and good-looking. We met at Starbuck's and appeared to hit it off immediately. He asked whether I liked to travel, and I replied yes. He announced, "I'm very adventurous. I plan to climb Machu Picchu this year and make a pilgrimage to India next year. I want to buy a small RV and travel all over North and South America. Does that sound like fun to you?"

Startled, I replied, "Uh, not really. I'm more a hotel kind of gal, not really interested in visiting third-world countries or camping." When we parted, he gave me a big hug and said we would get together soon. The next day I received an email saying we were not a match and wishing me luck. I can't say I was surprised.

Then an 85-year-old retired physician who lives 100 miles away in Santa Barbara emailed to say distance wasn't a problem. If we clicked, he would gladly move to Paso Robles. Shaking my head, I quickly hit delete.

I began to think that Match probably wasn't the place to find the companion I desired. I had one month until my subscription expired. One morning I saw a new profile that piqued my interest. He was age appropriate, lived within my county, shared a number of my interests, and seemed to possess a sense of humor. He had a slightly impish grin, and I liked the direct gaze of his dark eyes. I vacated my comfort zone and "liked" him; I included an email complimenting his thoughtful profile. He responded immediately and arranged a meeting that weekend.

We met at a coffee shop in San Luis Obispo. After chatting for two hours, he said, "I think we really hit it off; would you like to have lunch with me at the Madonna Inn next weekend?"

"Sure," I replied with my widest smile. His easygoing manner and sense of humor relaxed me. He appeared to have a curious mind and many interests and friends—another plus. He said he was close to his two adult children who lived on their own. Bingo!

Because he is still employed and we live forty-five miles apart, we only see each other on weekends. We have worked out a pattern of alternating weekends at each other's homes. We enjoy our mutual interests in long walks, word games, dining out, and watching old films. We find the same situations funny, so we laugh often.

*With my match—Frank—at the coast*

I think it's possible that I have now become the someone-who-someone-else-knows, the person who met her match online.

# Rules of Engagement

*By Martha Staib*

By the mid 1960s, America was in a war 6,000 miles away in the rice paddies and jungles of Viet Nam. War was being waged at home, as well, in protest marches against the unpopular war. Sometimes violence erupted in the streets of San Francisco. Young people were crying, "Make love, not war!" and staging sit-ins at the Berkeley campus nearby. I was attending Oakland High School and found myself in the middle of a cultural revolution.

Integration laws passed in the mid-1960s, with all their good intentions, meant that black students from the flatlands of Oakland were bussed to the all-white Skyline High School in the Oakland Hills to improve their access to public services and achieve equality in education. At Oakland High School we began to celebrate diversity and ethnic identity by starting school clubs that reflected our ethnic heritage. The search for a tribal identity was growing stronger every day, conflicting with calls for unity.

I had grown up among a rainbow of skin colors in elementary school, but now society was telling me I was different because I was white. Some friends no longer acknowledged me in the hallways. Students I had never met looked at me with hate in their eyes. We were all caught up in this social and cultural revolution. I found myself without a road map to guide me through the maze.

Racial and cultural divides also created a dating abyss. Blacks weren't allowed to date whites and vice versa. The same was true for children of Chinese and Japanese immigrants, rival cultures long before their families moved to the Bay Area. I had attended junior high school with a boy whose ancestry was Japanese. He was in several of my classes, and we became friends. He played electric guitar, wrestled, and was funny and sweet. He was also smart enough to snag a four-year scholarship to the Air Force Academy a few years later.

My mother, however, saw him only as a Japanese immigrant. She made it clear I would not be allowed to date him. He was one of several potential suitors that my mother crossed off the list. Her goal: to find me a nice White Anglo-Saxon Protestant (WASP) from a family with good economic and social standing—a tall order for anyone going to school in the flatlands of Oakland. It was OK for me to have friends of other races and ethnicities in grade school, but I couldn't date them in high school. I knew why my mother wanted me to have a comfortable, conforming future, but I still resented her control. I wanted to make my own choices.

I had always been interested in different cultures. One day I hoped to become a foreign exchange student, like the four exchange students who attended our high school in 1967. They had become my friends. That same year, I became the president of the high school student exchange club and spearheaded the fundraising events for the year. We had a successful pancake breakfast in the winter, after weeks of soliciting groceries from local stores and pleading for donations, as well as school-wide doughnut and Christmas card sales.

The following spring, the club hosted a first-ever All-City High School Battle of the Bands. We invited bands from each of the six high schools in Oakland to raise the roof of the auditorium and stimulate our fundraising efforts. Little did I know it would truly turn into a battle.

We sold tickets that released over 500 students from fourth-period classes, so the auditorium was packed. The bands began playing a little late, but soon one band after another played their songs to the cheers of the crowd. Then it came time for the final act, the band from the all-black high school in West Oakland. They were halfway through their last song when the bell rang for fifth period. A teacher stepped onstage and closed the curtain on the band while they were still playing! The band was livid, and so was the crowd. Students booed and yelled, and then they threw whatever was handy. No one left the auditorium. Oh my God, I thought to myself. I could feel the tension escalating as I sat in the audience with everyone else. Over the loudspeaker, an administrator announced, "Everyone get to class!"

Crowds of students ran through the school hallways, kicking over trash cans, littering the floors, and yelling for those still in class to join them. I was stunned. Pandemonium continued until an administrator announced that school was dismissed early due to the disruption. I couldn't wait to run home and hide. Later I wondered if all the visiting bands had returned home safely.

The next day the school was still in disrepair, and more groups of students continued to protest what they perceived as an intentional act of disrespect towards the black community. My mother, a woman who believed I should be in school every day regardless, said, "Marty, I think you better get out of town for the day until things cool down." She thought I could be a target since I was white and helped plan the fundraiser.

I had never seen my mother so scared for me. Shaken, I skipped school that day and stayed with a friend out of town. All the weeks of planning the event, along with my heavy class load and preparations for a water ballet solo, had left me exhausted. The next day I landed in the hospital with pneumonia. I never found out what the school administration did to resolve the unrest, if anything.

When I returned to school weeks later, I became more determined than ever to work within the school student government, building bridges instead of walls, to celebrate both diversity and our common humanity. With the help of family and friends, I was the first girl elected Vice President of the student body in the fall of 1968.

That fall I helped coordinate a school exchange with students from Oakland Technical High School. I shadowed Carl, a member of their student government, and then he shadowed me at Oakland High. As we toured our respective schools, we asked questions and learned how to improve our schools. Despite our ethnic and socio-economic differences, we became friends and kept in touch for years.

In November, I was accepted as a foreign exchange student in Sao Paulo, Brazil, for the coming year. I had achieved my goal. In 1969, I left

*Challenges*

my friends at Oakland High School behind to experience other cultures first hand.

*A 1970 yearbook photo of seniors cheering for the football team*

# Sibling Rivalry

*By Eileen O'Grady*

"I just got a new computer," my brother John bragged. "It does everything."

"Really," I replied. "I just got one too."

"What kind?"

"A PC."

"Mine's a Mac. They're much better."

"John," I sighed. "We don't have to do this. We're adults now."

"Yeah, but how much RAM do you have?"

Why are so many conversations with my younger brother similar to this exchange from 1998? I don't want to play this game. It's not that I don't want to lose; I don't even want to win. I want something completely different—a mature relationship.

Our father was a widower with two sons when he married my mother. I was her first-born; John arrived two years later. Maybe birth order dictated our childhood roles. I was a chronic overachiever. But graduating at the top of my classes in high school and college provided short-lived satisfaction. I decided to become a teacher and a mother, so I could nurture others—much more rewarding to me than awards and recognition.

My brother John was the class clown, a gregarious underachiever. As his escapades became more flagrant, he barely graduated from high school. College was a stretch—a long one. By the time he graduated, he was married, working full-time, and planning to attend law school. Eventually he became a founding partner in a Chicago law firm. He had

*Challenges*

transformed himself from aimless jokester into focused professional. His take-no-prisoners style became an asset for marketing legal services.

Whenever I travel to Chicago, John hosts a family get-together where he grills, bakes, pours wine, and invites our siblings and their children to attend. These large gatherings occur in the same neighborhood where our mother grew up. I appreciate John's efforts to be hospitable, a family trait we both learned in childhood, and I enjoy these rare opportunities to reconnect with family members I seldom see.

But these family get-togethers often deteriorate as John turns conversations into monologues. One occasion replays in my memory like a worn-out VHS tape. Fueled by alcohol, John bragged about his latest legal article, the journal prominent on his coffee table. His booming voice echoed off the living room walls, silencing other conversations. Later, he branched out, adopting another familiar role—the proud father who lives vicariously through his son's medals and ribbons. They too were on display.

Still later that same evening, after many guests had left, and John had consumed even more alcohol, he turned on me. In a loud, threatening voice, he asked, "Where are your articles? You are so average."

I turned away in silence, too stunned and hurt to even reply. For a few minutes I didn't know where I was. Why, during a family event, would he lash out at me? How was I, the supportive sister, transformed into a convenient target?

Eventually I realized that John was still trying to vanquish his presumed rivals, including me—to be smarter, more accomplished, more acquisitive. If it were anyone else, I'd take a lengthy sabbatical from this relationship. But we have grieved together through the tragedy of our mother's sudden death at age 52. And we've celebrated at family weddings and graduations. I still recall his eagerness to attend my daughter's wedding and the food he brought from Chicago to share with us.

A few years later, I invited John and his family to celebrate Christmas at my home in California. I figured his previous attack had been a once-in-a-lifetime event. Surrounded by his children and mine at the dinner table, he waited until I was in the kitchen clearing plates, and then he launched into yet another tale about how superior he is to me. Everyone at the table was shocked into silence. I could only hear snatches of his taunt from the kitchen, but I recognized the attack. And I couldn't blame his alcohol consumption. I had to respond.

"What's the matter, John?" I asked as I returned to the dining table. "Are you feeling insecure again?" No one spoke for several minutes; finally someone changed the topic.

Wary of encounters like this, I have kept my distance. Since I live 2000 miles away from him, it's easy. We talk on the phone occasionally, mostly about family. Sometimes he reminisces about childhood events.

A couple of years ago I decided it was safe to invite him and his wife to visit us again. If they flew out in mid-August, we could attend a winemaker dinner at one of our local wineries. A California wine event would be a unique opportunity for them. After he agreed to come, I wondered if I'd made a mistake.

My husband and I drove to the small airport in San Luis Obispo to pick them up. As we stood outside the chain-link fence, we watched their plane land and taxi to a stop. The door opened and a heavyset older man walked slowly down the ramp. It was my brother. I kept watching; my childhood nemesis and adult antagonist had now become weak and vulnerable.

*With my brother John in 1954*

As the weekend progressed, we laughed and cooked together, freed, at least for a few days, of the burdens of the past. He ordered a limousine to take us to the winery dinner Saturday night, and he insisted that we stop at In-and-Out Burger on

*Challenges*

the way home. In between we enjoyed a multi-course dinner and delicious wines in a movie-perfect setting: hilltop views of the vineyards in the foreground and the Santa Lucia Mountains in the distance.

Looking back, I'm glad I reached out to him. Sometimes, if we muster the strength to look beyond the scars from the past, we can begin again. We can focus on the loving occasions we once shared. We can become siblings without the rivalry.

# The Second Paycheck

*By Martha Staib*

"What do you mean you want to raise my rent?" I exclaimed to my landlord. "We just moved in last month!" I didn't know anything about renters' rights but raising the rent after only one month sounded shady. I bluffed my way through the conversation by pointing out it was nothing short of false advertising. He relented and kept the rent we had agreed on. Then he raised it twelve months later. Between school loans and the cost of raising two teenage daughters on my starting pay from the state hospital, I was constantly finding "more month at the end of my money."

My supervisor at the hospital agreed to let me work four ten-hour days each week, an arrangement that left me free on Fridays. I found a one-day-a-week clinical nutrition job at a community hospital about forty miles from home. Soon I was driving south each Friday on Highway 101. The combination of inpatient assessments and outpatient counseling offered a nice change from my work with mentally ill patients at the state hospital, and the second paycheck covered most of my outstanding bills. But it was soon obvious that I was missing out at home. School field trips, girls' basketball and volleyball games, and other school activities had taken a back seat, along with dinner and time together. I felt like a juggler with too many balls in the air.

I knew other health specialists and medical personnel from the state hospital who were assigned to an Army Reserve hospital unit in southern California, so I decided to investigate the Army Reserves. A job like that would allow me to return to a regular work week, earn enough extra money to pay for my rent increase, and be home more with the girls. I saw it as a way to fill in the financial gaps until my girls graduated from school.

A doctor who worked with me at the hospital had joined the Army Reserves after ten years of active duty. When I asked him about the risk of being called up, he smiled and said, "Our unit hasn't been activated since World War II!" His response eased my mind about the possibility of having to leave the girls to go fight in a war. And so, at the age of 38, I joined the Army Reserves Medical Specialist Corps. A federal hiring freeze was in effect when I finished my military in-processing, so I was officially only "attached" to the hospital unit and not assigned. The freeze meant I would not be paid for the monthly drills initially, but it was expected to be lifted soon.

The closest hospital unit was located in Ventura, so I drove 150 miles south after work on Friday night and returned late on Sunday. On drill weekends we started with morning roll call and then tried to march in formation around the indoor armory hall. "Huuuw rah, Drill Sergeant," we called out as we stumbled through the drills. We looked more like Keystone Cops than the U.S. Army as we turned the wrong way and bumped into each other. The drill sergeant rolled his eyes and gritted his teeth.

The doctors and nurses left to work in an offsite clinic while the rest of the medical specialists worked in the armory building. My duties as a first lieutenant were to oversee the weight control program for the reserve personnel and to attend officer training classes. I spent most of my time walking around the armory wearing my Class B skirt and blouse uniform, carrying a clipboard, and trying to look busy.

I enjoyed my monthly "me-time" weekends but worried about leaving my daughters at home. Jennifer was becoming moody and irritable, and I wasn't sure if she was exhibiting normal teenage behavior or something more troubling. As teenagers, my girls were old enough to take care of themselves for a day or two, but occasionally they got into fights. I never knew what I would be walking into when I came home. Once I found a shoe print on the ceiling of the living room which no one could explain. Fortunately, they were always happy to see me when I arrived home from drill weekends.

When Iraq invaded Kuwait in 1990, the United States geared up to support Saudi Arabia by preparing active duty personnel for combat in Operation Desert Shield. Soon the government realized they could not send reserve officers abroad to back up active duty officers if they had not even completed basic training. My mother volunteered to drive down from the Bay Area and stay with the girls after I received orders to complete my basic training. And so I found myself, along with hundreds of other medical personnel, at Fort Sam Houston, Texas, for a two-week crash course in all aspects of the military: map reading, weapons, and military organization. At Fort Sam Houston I learned how to speak army lingo, to salute, and to march confidently in my new camouflage Battle Dress Uniforms (BDUs), complete with heavy, black combat boots.

By the second week of training, rumors spread as reserve units were called up for Operation Desert Storm. "Who will be called up next?" we asked. "Where will we be sent?" By the end of intense basic training, I heard that MY reserve unit had been activated. My stomach churned as I tried to devise a plan for someone to care for my girls while I was on active duty. No way would my mother be able to handle two teenagers for long. Because I was not officially assigned to the unit, I was then told I would not be called up with the rest of my fellow officers. A huge load lifted off my back as I sank into a chair and silently gave thanks to the hiring-freeze gods. I felt a little guilty that others in my unit were being sent directly to active duty.

*Lunch break at Fort Sam Houston during my Army Reserves basic training*

As I arranged to return to California, I realized that working in a state hospital wasn't so bad after all. I looked forward to being back home in my normal routine.

Despite the 12–14-hour-long training days, I had enjoyed my time in basic training. I was able to hone a few of the survival skills I had learned during my Girl Scout camping days. Balancing work and home life had always been a challenge, but now I knew this second job would make life easier for us all.

# A World of Hurt?

*By Eileen O'Grady*

Cloaked in ambivalence, I entered the small second-floor waiting room of the pain management clinic. I completed the paperwork the receptionist gave me and took a chair. A woman seated nearby was connected to an oxygen tank. Another chatted about opioids with a man who entered. I felt like a fraud. I could breathe without help, and the strongest pain medication I'd taken was Aleve. What was I doing here?

For 15 years, after moving to California, I enjoyed jazz and tap lessons and performed in annual recitals. I took long walks and hiked occasionally. But, during a late summer hike six months earlier, I strained a muscle. Now I could no longer dance at all. I tried physical therapy for several months. The heat and massages felt great, but some of the prescribed exercises produced painful flare-ups. And I could hardly walk for weeks after a brief encounter with a stationary bike.

Climbing stairs had become a form of torture. I tried leading with my left leg instead of alternating since the pain was on my right side. At the grocery store, I divided the packages into increasing numbers of bags so I could lift them. I bought milk by the half gallon, instead of the gallon, and smaller sizes of laundry detergent. I skipped meetings if the location had too many stairs. I tried to focus on what I could still do. I could read and write. I could knit. I could cook, as long as I didn't stand too long. But on many days I wanted my old life back.

When physical therapy failed, my doctor ordered an MRI. "You have bulging discs," the nurse said when she called with the results. " You're not a candidate for surgery, but we can refer you to a pain specialist." I was relieved to have a diagnosis, glad that I would not need surgery, but still troubled. I was gaining weight from a lack of exercise, and my blood pressure was rising. I needed the referral.

While I waited for an appointment, I consulted friends and acquaintances familiar with back pain. They were easy to find. At Trader Joe's I saw Steve, a friend whose wife had recently had back surgery. Steve had back issues himself but couldn't tolerate anything stronger than Tylenol. My best "street source" was Judie, my dance buddy. She suggested a range of remedies from Lidocaine patches to anti-depressants. She had tried most of them herself with mixed results.

After an hour-long wait, I was ushered into an examining room at the clinic. The doctor asked me a series of questions while his assistant took notes on a laptop. Then he tested my legs to see how much pressure I could resist. "You've lost a lot of strength on your right side," he said. Should I be relieved that the specialist took me seriously? Or alarmed by my weakness? My right side had always been stronger than my left side.

"I recommend an epidural steroid injection. You don't have to put up with this," he concluded, his eyes compassionate. "Your insurance will cover it."

"How long will I have relief?"

"The average is two months."

"I need to think about it." Two months didn't sound very long.

"Google it. And come back in a month."

I left uncertain. Fueled by ibuprofen, I began taking short walks around the neighborhood. Some days I felt better afterwards; some days I felt worse. I decided to return to my low-impact Jazzercise classes. My friends greeted me warmly when I arrived; I'd been absent for six months. My right leg felt wobbly, so I moved slowly, ignoring the Aerobic Annies on the side of the room. As the tempo of the music increased, I coaxed my leg to move faster. I felt as if I might stumble and fall. Exhausted, I left early.

After several weeks of light workouts, I wanted more, so I scheduled the epidural procedure. My husband dropped me off at the surgery center and returned after the anesthesia had worn off. I was at Jazzercise the next day. The pain in my back and hip was gone. The knee pain remained, but it was manageable. Gradually I exercised at higher levels and took faster walks. Two months later I had a second injection. The knee pain disappeared too.

With steroids blanketing my nerves, I flew to Chicago in August to celebrate my 50th wedding anniversary. My husband Dan and I had met at a parochial school in third grade, dated in college, and married after graduation. Many of our family members still lived in the Chicago area. We had reserved a room at a French restaurant in Lincoln Park, near our daughter's home.

*Chicago's historic Water Tower—from our hotel room in 2018*

On the night of our anniversary party, we greeted friends and family members from all over the country. We sipped champagne and nibbled on chilled shrimp appetizers in the restaurant's spacious lobby. We moved inside to dine on steak or salmon. Each course was elegant. French wines smoothed over conversational gaps. Pain-free, I celebrated without distractions. I laughed with people I have loved for decades.

After the party, I inhaled my hometown like a tourist. Dan and I frolicked with our granddaughter at the fountain in Millennium Park. We strolled from our hotel near Chicago's historic Water Tower to shops and restaurants along Michigan Avenue. It all felt like a miracle.

After I returned home, I heard a report on NPR that compared pain management to a new frontier in medicine. I know my relief is temporary; my bulging discs remain. But chronic pain awakened me to the privilege of mobility. Now, when I am able to dance, I sing too. When I play with my granddaughter, I giggle. And when I spend an afternoon preparing a special dinner for my husband of fifty years, I light candles. It's a brave new world, and I'm eager to celebrate every miracle I can.

# My Stepmother

*By Martha Staib*

As I watch Kathryn lying in a nursing home bed, I realize I have had a stepmother for fifty years. The mood is somber, the darkened room quiet except for the rhythmic pumping of the oxygen condenser. Kathryn awakens and looks up at me. I say, "Hi."

"I wish I was!" she replies.

Kathryn Kelley was completely different from my serious, intellectual parents. When I first met her, she was 42 years old, tall and slender, with short, wavy dark brown hair. She smoked cigarettes and those small cigars called tiparillos. She drank to excess and told hilarious stories. Dad was enchanted by this woman whom he had met at the office. She was everything he wasn't. He could live his life vicariously through her misadventures growing up in Oklahoma in the 1930s, serving in the Marine Corps during WW II, and cruising across the Atlantic on the Queen Elizabeth 2 in the 1960s.

I met Kathryn in 1964 when Dad, who had separated from my mom, took my brother Bob and me to visit her in San Francisco. We arrived at her apartment near Ghirardelli Square and went bowling in Chinatown. We quickly realized that none of us could bowl very well, so that was the last time we went bowling together. We tried tennis next. I brought along a girlfriend, and we played doubles until one serve skimmed over the net and accidentally smacked Kathryn right in the mouth. That was the end of tennis.

The last "bonding" activity was backpacking in the Sierras. That too became a disaster as Bob and I hiked ahead, intentionally leaving Dad and Kathryn in the dust. No more backpacking trips after that. For decades Kathryn and I maintained a polite but reserved relationship. I let her know she was not my mother, and she reminded me in many ways that all we had in common was my father.

As a teenager, I found it difficult to give up the idea that my parents were not going to be reunited. As an adult, I married, had children, divorced, and returned to school before starting a career. I was much too busy to get to know Kathryn, except for occasional holiday visits. It took me about forty years to start to appreciate Kathryn as a real person with a real history.

Her own childhood had not been easy. Her mother married right out of high school and gave birth to five children in the next seven years. Kathryn was farmed out to her grandmother from the age of two until she was ten because her mother could not cope with so many young children. Kathryn was a daydreamer, but she did graduate from high school and attend college, where she discovered a passion for painting. When she decided to leave home, her mother said, "Fine, whatever, just leave that painting of the violinist here with me."

In 1943, Kathryn left college to help the war effort by joining the Marine Corps Women's Reserve. Her mother was upset by her decision, but her father proudly displayed another star in their front window. He told other residents of Sapulpa, Oklahoma, that they had three children in the military, Kathryn and her brothers Jim and Tom. She worked as a secretary at Camp Pendleton. Eventually she returned to California after finishing college in Oklahoma.

After Dad and Kathryn married, Kathryn was excited when Dad's work transferred them to Brussels in 1970; she was looking forward to learning French. While living in Europe, she contracted hepatitis A and was bed-ridden for six months. A year before that, she was diagnosed with breast cancer and had a total mastectomy. Despite these setbacks, she traveled throughout Europe. She loved their three-year stay in Belgium, always up for another adventure.

Kathryn learned to play golf—cautiously because of the muscle loss and brittle ribs from cancer surgery and radiation. She excelled at golf and continued to play through two knee replacements in her 70s, another total mastectomy in her 80s, and a heart valve replacement at the age of 90. She was disappointed when she left the women's 18-hole golf group and joined the 9-hole group at the age of 91, but she readily admitted it was time.

At some point in our relationship, I managed to smile, not grimace, when Kathryn, who never really liked to cook, told my father, "Honey, I married you for better or worse, but not for lunch." At the age of 94, when she broke her leg and wound up in the nursing home, her sense of humor was stronger than ever. From Kathryn I learned that life is not meant to be taken too seriously.

Whenever I visited her at the nursing home, Kathryn told me how much she appreciated me; she introduced me to others as her daughter. I was surprised and flattered each time. Although she died the following summer, I heard Kathryn's voice in my mind after my own knee replacement. She was saying, "Get up. Get moving and get over it!"

Faith, hope, and a good sense of humor had carried her through the Dust Bowl of the 30s, WW II in the 40s, a new career in a new state in the 50s, and life with my family for the next fifty years. It took me a long time to recognize her many virtues. I want to tell her, "Thank you, Kathryn."

*Kathryn in her golfing attire, next to her own golf cart*

# Losses

"What we have once enjoyed deeply we can never lose. All that we love deeply becomes a part of us."

---

*Helen Keller*

# Forgiving Dad

By Myra Lathrop

A caregiver opened the door to a modern tract home, now a board and care facility in Mission Viejo. He smiled, introducing himself as Tony. "I'm Myra, and this is my husband, Sonny," I replied with a shaky voice. He led us through a cheerful living room where residents were watching TV or dozing with blankets on their laps.

Tony opened the door to a sun porch where Dad sat in a wheelchair with both legs elevated and wrapped. He looked older and smaller since I had last seen him a few years earlier. The morning sun streamed through the enclosed porch, a lawn and garden beyond it.

"Hi, Dad," I whispered, not wanting to startle him. His head bobbed and turned toward my voice.

"Myra?" Then he smiled, and I gave him a gentle hug and a kiss on his cheek.

"Dad, this is my husband, Sonny. I got married a year ago." Dad extended an age-spotted hand. Sonny shook it and said he was happy to meet him.

I had not seen or spoken to my father for over three years. The last time we saw one another, in 1998, he had abruptly left a facility I had found for him. Somehow he had moved himself into an independent living residence without telling me. He had incipient dementia exacerbated by alcoholism, so I had been assisting him with his finances and other issues..

Dad had always been difficult, if loving, under the best of circumstances, but in the throes of dementia, he had become impossible. At our last visit, he screamed hateful accusations at me; then he told me he was getting married, for the fifth time, to a woman he had just met at an A.A. meeting.

"I don't need your help anymore; you never loved me anyway," he yelled. As I left his room in tears, I thought I would never see him again. I was angry and hurt by his vitriol.

Over the years, I had been on the receiving end of much of his fury. One time he came over for a Father's Day brunch. We were drinking champagne when he blurted out, "I have a bone to pick with you." He proceeded to rant about some inconsequential incident that occurred fifteen years prior, an incident which I could not even recall.

Any political discussion set him off into a tirade, neck flushing crimson and eyes bulging. "Reagan and his cohorts are a bunch of fascists. You'll see, the middle class will disappear in the next thirty years." I knew better than to utter one word, or he would argue all afternoon. The force of his ire seemed outsized and too often projected onto me, his older child.

Two years after his last tirade, the phone rang as I was preparing dinner. "Do you know Ted Coodley?" a Laguna Beach police officer asked.

"Yes, that's my dad. Is he O.K.?"

"Do you know a woman named Brenda? She and your dad were married."

"No, I don't know Brenda. Why are you asking?"

"Your dad has filed a report with us. Apparently she sold his condo and his car, cashed out his bank accounts, maxed out his credit cards, and then left in the middle of the night. She is a well-known grifter in this area who preys on lonely older men."

"Where is he now?" I inquired.

"He lives in an apartment in Laguna and has a caregiver."

I thanked the officer and hung up the phone, determined not to become entangled in my dad's life again. I had not forgiven him for the nasty tirade at our last encounter. He had a caregiver; he would have to figure it out.

About a year after the call, Dad's caregiver Jose contacted me. He told me Dad was in a board and care facility. He thought I should visit as soon as possible.

I was reluctant, but Sonny encouraged me. "I think it's important that you visit him. If he dies, and you don't make peace, you'll regret it. Let me go with you."

The afternoon visit in the sun porch had a surreal quality about it. Dad was a much different version of his former self. He had been a passionate man, romantic, political, argumentative, artistic. He now appeared subdued and even funny, trying his best to entertain and amuse us.

"Honey bunch, I met Grandma last night for dinner downtown. We went to Taix, the French place." His mother had died nearly thirty years before.

"Oh, how is she, Dad? Was the food good?"

"She's fine, the same as always." He broke into a smile, and I was unsure whether he was testing me or really believed he had had dinner with Grandma.

"How is everyone?" he asked.

"Fine. Josh is doing well, and Jake is growing fast." I wasn't sure whether he remembered his grandson and great-grandson. "Dad, I was telling Sonny that you have been married five times. Do you remember all your wives?" He nodded, grinning.

"How many children do you have?"

"Two," he replied.

"What are their names?"

"Joel and Myra," he answered, proud of himself.

"And who was your favorite wife?"

"Your mother, of course," he retorted sheepishly. The three of us laughed. Dad told us stories from his past, except for him they occurred in the present. He described movie locations where he had worked as a make-up artist and arguments he had had with a director. His manner was completely different from the one I had known all my life. He was light-hearted, almost joyful as he spun stories and checked to see whether we were enjoying them.

After several hours, I told him we had to leave but that we would return the following Sunday. I gave him a kiss, and then as Sonny was shaking his hand, my dad looked him in the eye and exclaimed, "Take care of Wild Thing!" I turned around, laughing as he winked at me.

On the way home, I told Sonny that I couldn't believe the change dementia had wrought. The sweet tenderness he displayed that day reminded me of his gentler qualities. I recalled that he could be loving, affectionate, and supportive. He encouraged me to play classical guitar and take modern and flamenco dance lessons. He often told me I was smart and pretty, and his warm hugs always included "I love you, Honey Bunch."

The next Sunday when we visited Dad, he was silent and unsmiling. I did all the talking while I held his hand. He had experienced several mini-strokes, and his kidneys were failing. His caregivers informed me that he was fading quickly.

When I hugged him good-bye, I told him he had been a good dad and said I loved him.

A week later I was identifying his body in the basement of the Laguna Beach Hospital. An orderly pulled back the sheet, and I moved forward to kiss him on his cold forehead. I told him I loved him one last time. Sonny and I walked out into the sunlight, and although I was sad, I felt at peace.

It took me over fifty years to see my dad as human and not just a parent. Now, when I think about him, I remember the severe case of whooping cough I had

*Dad and I, 1953*

at age five. He built a tent out of a sheet and put a vaporizer inside to aid my breathing. Then he joined me in the steam and drew cartoons on a blackboard while he told me silly stories. And I relaxed and breathed more easily.

# Homecoming

*By Liz Helgerson*

Everyone was gathered at the house that my father, son of a carpenter, had built for us sixteen years earlier. Straightforward and modest like my parents, the house lacked fantasy, but made up for it in practicality—two bedrooms and a bath on the first floor, along with an L-shaped living and dining room surrounding the square kitchen. In later years, Dad had finished a rec room in the basement and a bedroom for Margaret and me on the second floor—the latter necessitated by the surprise late arrival of my little sister Barbara, eleven years my junior.

Our front door was centered on the façade. Upon entering, guests found a coat closet on the left and a room divider on the right. It was South Dakota, after all, so it was important to deal with coats and the stiff cold that poured in whenever the door opened in winter. My mother's spinet piano, which served to separate living room and entry hall, was the first thing guests saw, along with the family's one art treasure—one of Oscar Howe's earliest abstract watercolors of Sioux Indian dancers. The room was decorated in pastel greens, with flowered prints on the upholstered furniture, giving it a warm and comfortable air. Dining table, hutch, and side tables were cherry with a shiny finish typical of the Early American style so popular at that time. It was, all in all, appropriate for a family of our station, surprising only because Dad's large collection of books was not displayed in the living room.

South- and west-facing windows let in the late afternoon sun on this particularly pretty spring day. In fact, because of the size of the gathered crowd, the windows had been opened to let in some breeze. Every chair was taken while other guests milled around the midday spread. Uncharacteristically, Mom was neither at the stove nor refilling platters.

Instead, she sat, wrapped in a stillness barely broken by her visitors' greetings.

I was in a fog, having arrived late the night before from the long trip home—Bordeaux to Paris to New York to Omaha to Vermillion. Though this was home, I couldn't shake a sense of dislocation. I'd been away for a whole junior year abroad. My sister Barbie was inches taller and acted much older; my high school friends had moved away; my fiancé seemed a total stranger. I was also spinning from my sister Margaret's early morning news. "We all met with Pastor Forbes yesterday," she stated firmly, "and we all agreed that it would be best for the family if you go ahead with your wedding next month. It will be good to have something positive to keep us busy." But what if that's not what I want? I thought it but failed to respond.

Never a social butterfly, I did my best to avoid engaging with anyone, but I did hear bits and pieces of the conversations around me. "I saw Everett hurrying across campus in his shirt sleeves, and I knew instantly something was very wrong. You know, he was never out of his office without his suit coat on." This was from Evelyn Cummins, mother of my best high school friend.

"Wasn't it wonderful how many people came to Ev's funeral?" I heard Dad's colleague, Tom Geary, say. "The church was completely full. Faculty were there in force, and even his students came. I know Kitty and the girls were proud to see how many people cared."

Doris Estee, another of Mom's good friends, was telling the whole story to some of the ladies from church– how Dad had rushed home on foot after experiencing the first pains of his heart attack, and how he asked Mom to drive him to the hospital about one mile away. "What makes it really sad," she related, "is that the initial tests at the hospital all looked fine. They just wanted to keep him for observation. Ev actually sent Kitty home so that she could cancel his classes and be there when Barbie returned from school. But—can you believe it?—when Kitty got home, the phone was already ringing. It was the hospital calling to say that Ev had died!"

"Oh my," someone said, "You mean she never even had a chance to say goodbye?"

I don't know how much Barbie, then eight years old, heard of these stories. She was at the gathering, having stayed home from the funeral itself. Since she had stated that she would rather not attend the funeral, the pastor and everyone else agreed that she shouldn't be pushed. This was easier at the time, I suppose, but it had set her outside the circle of mourners. It was hard to tell what she was feeling. More subdued and quieter than usual, she shed no tears. She simply moved away if anyone cried—especially when our mother lost control of her sobs.

The only one who seemed to bring Mom comfort was her brother, my uncle Tom. The adored youngest child (and only boy) in a family of girls, Uncle Tom was a successful chemist and manager working in the auto industry. At this moment, with Dad suddenly taken from us, he was forced to play the role of family patriarch. He did look the part in his dark funeral suit; most importantly, he seemed a center of calm in a world that had suddenly and madly tilted out of control.

Realizing that Barbie was being left to fend for herself, Uncle Tom engaged her in conversation. "So, Barbie," he asked, "how is school this year? Do you like your teacher?"

Barb lit up for the first time that day. She chatted away about her school work, her piano lessons, her friends. "And, do you know, Uncle Tom, I found a wild baby bunny! Her mother had gone away. Mom and Dad let me bring her home, and I've been taking care of her."

"Wow," he said. "That's got to be fun. Can I see her?" Barbie didn't have to be

Friend Barb, sister Marg, and I helped Dad build our home in 1949 asked twice. Off she ran to return moments later, proudly displaying her tiny pet.

The bunny, poor thing, was less than happy about a room full of strangers. She immediately jumped from Barbie's arms and hid under the sofa. Barbie tried to catch her, but only succeeded in chasing the more and more frightened animal from one hiding place to another. Others joined in. Pretty soon, we mourners were all laughing as the "catch the bunny" game spun on. It was Uncle Tom who unsurprisingly saved the day. Abandoning his suit coat, he got down on his hands and knees and recruited helpers to move Mom's stove just enough so that he could work his arm around to the back and capture Barb's bunny.

For a moment, as everyone laughed and cheered, it felt like home.

# Lost and Found

*By Eileen O'Grady*

When Allison called in 2018 to tell me her mother had died, I burst into tears.

Kathy and I met in first grade when my grandmother spotted a freckle-faced girl standing alone in front of our elementary school. It was the first day of school, and I didn't know anyone. Neither did Kathy.

During that school year and the ones that followed, bike-riding, reading, and dance lessons nurtured our friendship. Kathy was a much better athlete than I was, but our personalities meshed. We were even the same height, our birthdays just weeks apart. I developed a lisp during the school year, just like Kathy's. During the summer, my lisp disappeared. I seldom saw Kathy then.

After Kathy discovered the Mickey Mouse Club TV show in third grade, we both became dedicated viewers. Together we transformed our asphalt schoolyard—a blank space with no equipment whatsoever—into a stage where we could reprise the song-and-dance routines from the previous day's show. Other girls joined in. In the classroom, we slogged through endless drills, knowing we could become Mouseketeers at recess. Kathy was always Annette.

One day in fourth grade, Kathy decided we should run away to California and become real Mouseketeers. I hesitated. "We can stow away on an airplane," she suggested. I couldn't refuse. When the bell rang, instead of heading off in different directions, we left together, en route to Midway Airport where we'd hide on a plane bound for Los Angeles. We chatted with excitement for the first mile or so. By then the sun was sinking in the chilly November sky. When I stopped, Kathy urged me to continue. Tears formed in her eyes as I resisted.

Our parents banned the Mickey Mouse Club for a week after that episode, but our friendship persevered. We wrote mysteries, inspired by the Hardy Boys and Nancy Drew. Then Kathy discovered the Black Stallion stories. By seventh grade she was taking riding lessons. One Saturday she invited me to her stables to watch. Kathy mounted her horse while I sat nearby. I noticed her posture, her special riding clothes. She rode her horse around a ring, stopping and starting on command. She radiated confidence.

As eighth grade approached, disaster struck: a new highway claimed my house. The one my parents found to accommodate our multi-family household was located miles away, so I lost all my childhood landmarks. I clung to phone calls and infrequent sleepovers with Kathy, but sometimes she spoke about people I'd never met. Soon we both stopped calling. I made new friends, but they were never Kathy.

When I retired, I tried to find Kathy online. I quickly learned that she lived in Colorado. In just a few minutes on the phone, we bridged several decades. Kathy had become an avid skier during college. She and her husband Rob had moved to Colorado to be close to the slopes they loved. They owned a preschool and had a college-aged daughter named Allison.

"Do you travel?" she asked. I told her about trips to Europe we'd taken and visits to our daughter in New York City.

"What about you?"

"I don't travel," she replied. "I can't find substitutes." Her preschool provided year-round day care, so even her summers were committed.

We pasted emails into the gaps in our new relationship. I read lively descriptions of her school, the small mountain town she lived in, her daughter Allison. Kathy and Rob enjoyed dining at Mirabelle's, a local restaurant where they knew the owners. She sent scores of photos of Allison and their dog. Her life sounded idyllic at times; she seldom mentioned Rob's recovery from delicate back surgery. I remembered how, back in elementary school, she had never told me about her parents' divorce.

The following summer my husband Dan and I flew to Denver and rented a car for the two-hour drive to Avon, the town near Vail where

Kathy lived. When Kathy and I hugged, the years disappeared. We met Rob and Allison, visited the preschool Kathy directed, and dined at Mirabelle's together. We played with her Welsh corgi and hiked around the nearby hills.

When we invited them to visit us in California, Kathy agreed to come the following summer. She didn't fly, she said, so she would drive. Rob's back issues made it hard for him to travel, so she would come alone. We discussed the places we'd go to—Hearst Castle, local wineries, the ocean. A week before Kathy's arrival, she called to say she had anxiety attacks and couldn't come. I was so disappointed.

The following summer Kathy planned to visit again, this time with her daughter. Having Allison with her would relieve her anxiety, she said. We set a date, and I readied the guest room. But her attacks returned. Who was this Kathy? The girl I knew was determined, even fearless. Our emails dwindled. We needed more hooks to build a new relationship.

In 2014 Kathy and Rob sold their preschool and moved to northern Michigan where Allison had settled with her husband and their two boys. Kathy sounded excited about the move. They'd be close enough for frequent visits with their grandsons.

What she didn't tell me was that she had been diagnosed with lymphoma shortly before her move and refused conventional medical treatment. For several years, Allison said, Kathy had been in remission, but the tumors had returned the previous summer.

"She wanted to live long enough to see the boys in their Halloween costumes," Allison said. Kathy reached that goal—but not much more.

Allison and I spoke for 45 minutes. She told me about the accolades that had poured in from former students when they learned of Kathy's illness. She described her mother's last few days: her growing tumors, her attitude of acceptance, her peaceful death. We traded stories about the wonderful ways Kathy had graced our lives, and we shared our regret that the California trip had never materialized. I didn't tell Allison how much I missed the adventurous girl I once knew.

"I thought she told you about her illness when the lymphoma returned," Allison said. "I asked her to tell all her friends." But she hadn't told me. That was the Kathy I knew and loved, struggling with a terminal illness, but never wanting to burden others.

I felt devastated. I had lost Kathy when my family moved away from our original neighborhood. I lost her again—even after I had found her—when her anxiety intervened. When she died, I lost her forever.

A few days later I emailed Allison, thanking her for sharing so much about her mother's last years. Somehow she had sensed what I'd need to know. Then I replayed the childhood scenes I'd never forget: two slender girls on an asphalt playground, wearing Mickey Mouse ears and screaming in delight; the same girls in pink satin costumes, chatting before a dance recital. I heard our whispered conversations during a sleepover, my mother telling us firmly to go to sleep.

Because of Kathy, my otherwise lonely childhood sparkled. I'd never really lost her after all.

*School pictures of Kathy, on the left, and me, 1957*

*Losses*

# The Paddle Out

By Myra Lathrop

I awoke suddenly. Sun streamed through the blinds, and for a moment I forgot I was at my mother's house. Today is the day, I whispered to myself. At 10 a.m. fifty friends and relatives would gather at the jetty in Marina del Rey for my deceased husband Sonny's paddle out. I had attended a few of these beautiful celebrations of life, a tradition in the surfing community. Fellow surfers paddle out beyond the waves and hold hands in a circle. They share memories and then release the deceased person's ashes into the sea, followed by fresh flower leis. Then they paddle back to shore to celebrate their comrade's life.

Sonny battled malignant brain cancer for almost nine years, allowing us time to discuss his end-of-life wishes. He was firm about not wanting a funeral or memorial of any kind. His oldest son had died in an automobile crash years earlier, and he was still appalled by the elaborate and costly funeral his former wife insisted upon. "I just don't want that; it's such a waste. Please have me cremated and scatter my ashes in a pretty place," he said. He reaffirmed this wish several times over the years.

At one point I suggested a paddle out, led by my son Josh, a surfer in L.A., and Sonny's two sons. Sonny had been a master scuba diver and loved the ocean, so he said that would be something he'd like. "But no big party, just immediate family." I smiled, pleased with his concession. Simple and fitting, or so I thought at the time.

I had relayed Sonny's desire to both my son and my two stepsons, Loren, who lives in Nashville, and Ryan, who lives in New York City. They had no objections and appeared to accept their dad's wishes without question. But when he died in April, and I spoke with my stepsons about setting a date for the small ceremony, Ryan, erupted in a rage. "You can't

*Losses*

77

just have us. There are lots of people who knew and loved him. We need to have a big party in L.A. to celebrate his life. I want to knock back a few beers and tell stories about my dad with friends and family. We can have it at Alan's house (Sonny's best friend and long-time business partner). I know that's what my dad really wanted. He always loved a good party."

I was flabbergasted by his outburst. Unlike his older brother, Ryan had visited his dad in Paso Robles only a few times in nine years. His phone calls had been infrequent. "Look, Ryan, I know you are upset. This is a very emotional time for all of us, but please listen. I told you what his wishes were, and what you want is not what he wanted. He was adamant."

"No way! I need this. I'm calling Alan and making my own list of people, and you can have your paddle out with your family. You didn't know my dad the way I did." He hung up.

I burst into tears, shaky and scared, unsure about what to do. Within a few minutes, Loren called to tell me Ryan had spoken to him, terribly upset. "Loren, what should I do? I want to honor your dad's wishes; he didn't want a big bash."

"Are you sure that's what he really wanted? You know how my dad could be, kind of self-effacing, not always forthright with his wishes. Maybe we should read between the lines."

I couldn't believe Loren would even question what he knew to be true. He had been such a good friend and ally to me throughout his dad's illness. I felt betrayed and alone. Trying to remain composed, I replied, "I had hoped this would be smooth; you guys know that your dad hated any kind of dissension. This is exactly what he didn't want to happen. I intend to honor his wishes."

"Well, I guess we'll have two events. Ryan won't change his mind. I don't know whether we can fly across the country twice; it's expensive."

Exploding with pent-up anger I retorted, "You guys do what you want; I'm having a paddle out." Within hours, Alan called to say he was lending his home to Loren and Ryan for a celebration of life. He had known both boys since birth and felt he couldn't deny Ryan that request.

The date was set, the evites were going out the next day, and a caterer had been contacted.

I sank into depression and spent several sleepless nights ruminating over how to resolve this. I couldn't betray Sonny. How dare Ryan swoop in after all these years of absence and co-opt the plan. Why was I surprised? For Ryan, everything had been about him.

One morning, after tossing through the night, I gazed at our wedding photo in the hall and wished I could ask Sonny how to resolve the dilemma. I reflected on the man he had been. People often told me he was the best listener they had ever met. His relaxed, accepting demeanor encouraged both friends and business associates to open up to him with their stories and worries. He had the ability to impart insights and solutions with compassion. Several people confided that he had helped to change their lives in a significant way. He urged people to seek answers that included cooperation and reconciliation.

He was also the life of the party; he loved to plan and host events where food and liquor flowed, and friends talked, laughed, and danced for hours. Recalling who Sonny was led me to a solution that seemed right.

Excited, I dialed Ryan's number. "Yeah," he answered, in a wary voice.

"Ryan, I think I have a solution that will work for all of us. What if we combined the paddle out with a celebration of life? We could invite as many people as you like."

"But I already sent out the evites for an event at Alan's in three weeks," he snapped back.

"That's O.K. Just send me the list and emails, and I will take care of the change. After you and Josh and Loren paddle out with your dad's ashes, we will all go to a nearby restaurant for lunch. I will take care of it all. You just have to show up." My mouth felt like cotton waiting for his reply.

"O.K. Yeah, I think that would work." I could sense his tension easing.

"Wonderful; we'll do it at the end of June. I promise it will be everything you want it to be."

June 25 was a clear, sunny morning at the jetty as friends and family gathered with flowers, memories, and love. I felt the tension in my neck and stomach disappearing. Everyone had come to honor Sonny; he had touched each of them in some way. I felt joyful instead of sad, almost euphoric. I placed fresh orchid leis around the necks of our three sons and three grandchildren.

We sat in a semi-circle as people stood to share their memories of Sonny. We laughed and cried and then hugged and kissed one another. When Josh, Loren, and Ryan hopped onto their surfboards to paddle beyond the gentle waves with Sonny's ashes, the rest of the group walked to the water's edge to watch, snapping photos with their phones. The three men held hands, shared a few Sonny stories, and then released his ashes and the leis they had worn. Later, Josh said that Ryan and Loren told him he would always be a true brother to them. He, in turn, told them how much he loved their father. I hugged my son, unable to speak.

As we gathered for lunch at the restaurant on the beach, I caught Ryan's eye; he smiled and gave me a thumb's up. I imagined Sonny standing behind him, beaming with approval. I looked out the restaurant window at the summer light playing on the sparkling waves. I closed my eyes, took a deep breath, and relaxed into the rest of the afternoon. Ryan was right; this was just the kind of party Sonny would have loved.

*Sonny's Paddle Out, 2017*

*Losses*

# The Suede Vest

*By Martha Staib*

Early in January 2009, my daughter Jennifer called me from her father's hospital bed in Idaho. "He's in pain and the damn nurses won't give him any more morphine!" she yelled into the phone. I could tell Jennifer was at her wit's end. Her sister Carleen had just returned from visiting her father at Christmas. When Jennifer called, Carleen was staying with me and my second husband Ron in California before returning to Massachusetts. She and I looked at each other; we knew Jennifer needed our help.

The Weather Channel was reporting a massive winter storm gathering in the Northwest. Reluctantly, I booked a flight for the two of us for the next day. By the time we picked up our car in Spokane and headed south, we were in the midst of a snowstorm. Heavy SUVs and trucks around us skidded off the road, coming to rest on their side or overturned. No snowplows were in sight. I silently thanked God that Carleen, who had years of driving experience in New England winters, was at the wheel.

Looking out the window at the icy roads and pine trees, my mind wandered back to the early years of my first marriage. Jennifer was born in Sacramento in July of 1974, a year after Keith and I eloped. Most of Keith's relatives lived in the Sacramento area, so we were always welcomed for the holidays and family celebrations. My parents and I had reconciled our differences about my marriage for the sake of their first grandchild. Keith and I became apartment managers in Folsom, and I began night school. On our second wedding anniversary, I splurged and bought Keith a suede vest, a financial extravagance that seemed fitting.

Our future was looking bright; we had a steady income, and we'd become a family.

In 1976, we moved to Idaho, the state where Keith had grown up. Carleen was born in Nampa in August of that year, and we settled into the slower lifestyle. I learned to sew children's clothing and preserve the produce from our garden. Keith hunted pheasant in the fall and went ice fishing in the winter. In the spring our whole family picked wild asparagus along the abandoned railroad tracks, and in summer we camped in the mountains north of Boise. Keith spent many hours whirling his daughters around as airplanes, raking autumn leaves into tall piles so they could jump into them, and digging with them in the vegetable garden.

A few years later, I saw the cracks in our relationship. We had moved ten times in the first five years of marriage; Keith had left four jobs. He was accustomed to moving from one job to another every year or two; the pressure of being tied down to one job for the sake of a family and a mortgage had begun to wear him down. The girls were now in school, and I found work to help pay the bills, but it was all too much for Keith. After many heated arguments, slammed doors, and hurt feelings, we finally decided to end the marriage and go our separate ways.

Keith went back to being a drifter, and I returned with the girls to California for school and work. I hadn't kept in touch with him much after the divorce. When my daughters left home for college, they maintained a casual relationship with their father. He made brief appearances at their college graduations.

In 2008, we received word that Keith was terminally ill with lung cancer. The cancer had spread to his spine; he had only a short time to live. No other family members had shown up to support him, so the girls had flown to Idaho to take turns being with him. Now he lay dying in a Lewiston hospital bed, across the bridge from his home in a rundown trailer park.

It took us almost four hours to drive the stormy 100 miles that night; we arrived close to midnight. We rushed to the hospital to check on him. Then Carleen and I fell asleep in the lodging adjacent to the hospital that was reserved for families of cancer patients. Four hours later one of the hospital nuns awakened us to tell us that Keith had died. We returned to the hospital and gathered at his bedside as the girls said their final goodbyes. I knew then that this was why I had traveled through the winter storm—to be there for our daughters. My heart reached out to them as Carleen placed a pair of her hand-knit socks on his feet to keep him warm on his journey.

We spent that morning sharing stories about Keith over breakfast at a local restaurant. All three of us took turns laughing and crying into our coffees. "I remember camping along the Snake River in our tent. I fell into the river where we were fishing, and Dad had to pull me out!" Jennifer recalled. "He always had a sixth sense for where the fish were biting. I guess I got my love of fishing from him." They remembered his jokes, his smile, and the twinkle in his eye when he told them stories of his own youthful misadventures. I was glad that they were too young to recall the tension in our home during those final months before we separated.

Later that day, Jennifer returned to Sacramento. I accompanied Carleen as she made mortuary arrangements, closed his meager bank account, and cleaned out his one-bedroom trailer. In the trailer we found a copy of Carleen's new book. It was scheduled to be published later that year, but she had managed to give her father an autographed advance copy. In the book's introduction, she mentioned her parents who "went back to the land" in search of self-sufficiency and her fond memories of our family life in Idaho. Even though Keith was gone, he would live on in the hearts of my daughters.

As we looked into his closet, I noticed a suede vest hanging among the three or

*Celebrating Thanksgiving with Stepdad Howard, Keith and the girls in 1979*

four shirts he owned, the same one I had given him early in our marriage. I couldn't believe he had kept it for thirty years. Tears came to my eyes as I remembered those happier times when we lived together in Idaho, learning to parent our two beautiful daughters, and sharing our hopes and dreams with each other.

# The Long Slide

*By Marilyn Hamilton*

Two sisters born two years apart, Judie and I differed in our approaches to life. I was the quiet student who earned good grades and didn't want any trouble. She was the social one with lots of boyfriends and an adventurous, almost daring attitude. Mom would often say to Dad in frustration, "Dale, you talk to her. I can't get through."

I went to college and Judie married the same year. She was 17; Lee was four years older. They were a "hippie" couple, he with a curly beard, and she with long raven-colored hair parted in the middle. Like others in the late 60s, they drank alcohol and smoked marijuana.

In 1975 they moved to Enderby, British Colombia, in their Volkswagen bus. They planned to start a new business and build a home for their children, Mark and Tammy. Judie and I had been living in adjacent suburbs in southern California, so I was sad to see them move so far away. But I was also excited for them and their new adventure. Once Judie and Lee settled there, Enderby, nestled in the lakes and mountains of B.C., became a wonderful spot to vacation. During the day we enjoyed the outdoors; in the evening we talked, drank, and played darts at the local pub.

One night I received a call from Lee telling me Judie was drinking a lot, saying nonsensical things, and accusing him of affairs. He wondered if he should put her in the hospital. I was so alarmed that I told him I would drive there right away. I was in the first year of my Master's degree coursework in counseling and guidance, and I hoped I could help. I took along my children, Monty and Holly, in my little yellow 1979 Datsun.

I found the situation as troubling as I worried it might be. Judie told me that a person named Judy Dale was putting ideas in her head, and that Lee was trying to kill her. Her thoughts were disconnected, her associations loose, and she was conflating our dad's name, Dale, with this Judy Dale person. I racked my brain for ways to help. Logic and rational thought weren't working. Finally, I decided to get her out of the house.

We drove up north to Revelstoke, a lovely small town by a lake in the Canadian Rockies. We relaxed and, most importantly, didn't drink any alcohol. This seemed to help: Judie became herself again. When I mentioned counseling, she responded negatively. The kids and I stayed in Enderby for several more days. Judie was much more grounded, so we headed back to California. My mother and my step-dad Chuck were going to travel to B.C. later that summer. We hoped having family around would keep Judie stable.

Judie and Lee separated two years later after Judie became paranoid again. Her drinking continued. I saw it first-hand when she came to Monty's high school graduation. We held a party at home for him, and when I tasted her drink, it was pure vodka. "Judie, you need to think about A.A."

"No, I'm good," she replied. She laughed and became flirtatious around Monty's friends from high school, as if she were the same age.

Judie had a second chance at love when she married Helge, a Canadian of Swedish heritage. At six feet, six inches, he was more than a foot taller than she was. When Judie brought him to meet the family, he appeared to be a friendly guy with many stories and jokes to tell, most of them vulgar. Sadly, they each had found a drinking partner.

On one occasion, Judie called to tell me that Helge was abusive. I sent her information on domestic violence. I felt so helpless being so far away. I encouraged her to leave. In another phone call, she said she went to the police station because Helge was drunk. She wanted them to arrest him. Instead they put her in jail for the night.

When she called to say she had left Helge, I was relieved. I pleaded with her to come to California. "Stay with Bill and me, and we'll help you find work."

"No, Mark and Tammy are here," she replied. I recalled my mother's complaint that she could not get through to Judie. Now I couldn't either.

Judie and Helge reunited. In 1999, they joined us for Mother and Chuck's 25th anniversary. The entire family was cruising to Mexico to celebrate. I was shocked when I saw her again. She looked old, her long hair now a short blond bob. She seemed tired throughout the cruise.

Fast forward five years: Judie and I were discussing plans for Mom's 85th birthday. She sounded excited: she and Helge had bought a new car to drive to California. She also mentioned that she hadn't been sleeping well; her doctor had prescribed sleeping pills.

"Be careful with those," I admonished. "They can mess you up." I always felt anxious when I spoke to Judie.

I awoke the following Sunday with a strange feeling of stillness. The phone rang. It was Tammy.

"Mom is gone," she said.

"How?"

Tammy told me that Helge had risen early and gone for a hike. When he returned, he found Judie in bed, not breathing. Tammy was crying as she spoke. I was crying too. She said an autopsy had been ordered since her mother's death was suspicious. I discovered later that they had found an empty whiskey bottle near the bed and a near-empty bottle of sleeping pills.

*Judie and Lee in 1967*

Mom and I discussed Judie's death endlessly. Where was Helge? How could she be so excited about the trip coming up in a month but then overdose? So many questions, so much shock and disbelief. Six months later Canadian authorities ruled her death a suicide, a result of a lethal dose of sleeping pills and a blood alcohol level of 40 percent.

We all flew to Canada for Judie's memorial service. Helge was so emotional that Bill thought he felt guilty. Maybe he had said something to Judie that sent her over the edge. I wondered too. I spoke at the service, remembering Judie's life in Arcadia, California; her life with Lee and their children; her life with Helge. It was all I could do to speak, but I wanted to honor her memory and speak about the love we shared.

I still have unanswered questions. What was she thinking? Can a person commit suicide accidentally? I will never find the answers, but I know that she must have been in a place of pain she could not ease. Her burial site is a beautiful tree-shaded spot. I hope she's at rest now in her peaceful garden.

# An Ending

*By Liz Helgerson*

The sun bore down brutally on that June day, the way it can be in Kansas when everything is damp and even the concrete seems to sweat. To be out there in the middle of the day, breaking ground for a new garden, spoke of simple madness.

Perhaps I was already crazed that day. We had lived through quite a year. Doug and I had purchased and moved into a modest house in mid-May the year before, just before the birth of Laura, our second child. Doug was completing research for his Ph.D. dissertation in Clinical Psychology while he worked full-time at the local Community Mental Health Center. I kept busy as mother of an infant and a toddler, part-time graduate assistant instructor of French, and typist on Doug's dissertation. This was back in the days before text processing on a computer. In addition to typing the multiple review drafts required for his professors' approval, I had to meet the graduate school requirement for ten copies of the finished product—two originals with four carbon copies behind each of those. I passed many long nights at the typewriter after the kids went to sleep, having learned that it was easier to re-do the pages with errors than to correct those horrible carbon copies. Needless to say, I was NOT making much progress on my own dissertation in French Literature.

Despite the frenzied pace, we had survived the turmoil and political upheaval of the 60s and early 70s, had succeeded in our studies, and after 10 years as married students, our only student indebtedness was the National Defense Student Loan that I had used for a junior year in France. Doug had completed his dissertation; just weeks before he had marched in the graduation ceremony. We even had a little equity in our home and owned our car, a Datsun square-back that Doug was rescuing from rust rot and repainting with orange boat paint.

The only cloud in my skies: a growing awareness of distance between Doug and me. It had been a year of all work and no play. He spent less and less time at home, and we rarely did anything together just for fun. There was no extra money for babysitters or nights out; our best friends had moved away. That's why I had, the day before, convinced him to take a short day-trip to a lake in the area. As it turned out, that day had been no fun at all. It ended with a "trapped in the car" confrontation.

The trouble started when Doug said, "You know, I'm just not happy being a father, and I don't think I'm good at it either. I'm so impatient with Aaron," he continued, "and Laura is still mostly a chore." At first I listened and tried to be supportive. But I exploded when he said, "I just don't feel that I'm doing what I need for my own self-realization. I won't be any good to anybody else if I'm not being good to myself."

"Don't give me that psycho-babble," I angrily retorted. "Do you think I'm spending all day taking care of myself? This focus on your own happiness, it's just a way to glorify your selfishness."

The next day, things between us felt extra stiff, the house a prison. With kids down for a nap, I tried to attack the landscaping and put in a vegetable garden. I worked furiously at the earth, mixing purchased topsoil with the thick clay of our yard. Through memory's lens, I see the scene vividly – me, red in the face, covered in sweat, dirt smeared on my arms and legs. Doug approached with a guarded look on his face.

"I thought we'd planned to do this together," I said.

"I know," he replied, "but you know I just don't want to be here."

The emotional blow landed right in my stomach, doubling me over – raw grief as hot as the day. Doug just turned and walked away.

The rest of the day passed in pretended normalcy. I made supper; he cleaned the kitchen while I bathed the children and read stories; we both settled down with something to read. About 10:00 p.m., Doug rose and announced that he needed a pack of cigarettes. We had both quit smoking with Laura's arrival, but Doug had started again. It was another source of tension between us. As he explained it, his co-researcher was allergic to the smoke, so he could only indulge his habit at home.

The 15 minutes required for a run to the store came and went; the next minutes and hours passed slowly. Before he returned, I locked the door and went to bed.

It was almost 2:00 a.m. when his loud knocking shook me into motion for another confrontation.

"Where were you?"

"Just driving around and thinking."

"Thinking what?"

"I told you the truth earlier today. I just don't want to be here."

"Well," I said. "If that's the case, you are not welcome here. You should just go."

And he did.

Muggy heat still hung over town, stifling any sense of broken tension. Instead, the air was heavy with broken dreams. I spent the rest of the night throwing Doug's clothes and other possessions on the front lawn. The end had come. It didn't yet feel like a new beginning.

*The Beginning, 1968*

# Triumphs

"You struggle . . . again and again.
And then one day, you triumph."

––––––

*Kate Grace*

# A Rom-Com Courtship

*By Marilyn Hamilton*

I work at sorting Christmas card orders in the stationery department at Bullock's Department Store in Pasadena, a Christmas job I took after returning from a nearly year-long trip to Europe with my roommate. It's a fill-in job, so I don't feel like a leech living with my parents.

As I sit sorting the cards, I look up to see a tall, dark, handsome guy who is not a complete stranger. I recognize him as the older brother of JoAnn Hamilton, a girl I have known since elementary school. She and I were part of a carpooling group attending Mt. San Antonio College, but I had lost track of her. Now her brother, this hunky guy, asks me to coffee on our break. I accept.

"What are you doing at Bullock's?" I ask as we sip our coffees.

"Well, right now I am the box boy in stationery," he tells me with a grin. A little old for that, I think. But he adds, "I'm between jobs and living with my parents right now; I'll start airplane mechanic school in January."

"How is JoAnn?" I ask.

"Oh, do you know my sister?" I tell him I know her from high school and junior college. We make plans to have coffee again the next day. And the next day and the next. Then Bill starts coming to my house to pick me up in the morning, and we drive to work together every day.

One day after we finish our shift, he asks if I will help him pick out a Christmas gift for his girlfriend. Well, that seems odd, I think. We browse the ladies department, and he asks if I like this blouse or that, and I select one. The next day he hands me a nicely wrapped present and says it's a Christmas gift. There inside is the one I chose—a long-sleeved, embroidered cream-colored blouse.

"So, am I your girlfriend?"

" I hope so," he replies. I laugh, flustered but happy.

We go out on dates to dinner, to the movies, to the beach, and to meet his friends.

"Who are you going out with?" my mother asks me.

"Bill Hamilton."

"Oh, no, not Bill Hamilton!" Mom replies, sounding horrified.

"Why, what's wrong with that?"

Mom tells me Bill was a student in her Sunday School class at church, and he was a handful. Despite her misgivings, Bill and I continue dating. He calls and comes over even as flowers arrive for me from another guy I date.

"When I first saw you in Bullock's, I was dumbstruck, thinking this is the person I am going to marry," Bill tells me. Within a month he asks me to marry him. I stutter and avoid the answer despite the stars in my eyes. We drive up to Mt. Baldy one Saturday; on the way back I tell him who I would like for bridesmaids and what kind of flowers we'll carry.

"Does that mean you are saying yes?" Bill responds.

"Well, yes," I reply. I am nothing if not indirect.

This seems to be wedding season because in February, as we dine at a Japanese restaurant in Hollywood, he invites me to his friend Gail's wedding. It's in the Catholic church in Altadena, and I immediately like Mary, Gail's new bride. In early April we attend Bill's sister JoAnn's wedding. She and Hugh are married in the Presbyterian church in Arcadia in a lovely ceremony. I catch the bride's bouquet.

Two weeks later, on April 22, Bill stands tall and handsome in his dark suit, and I'm in my white satin brocade sheath, wearing a Jackie O pillbox hat. We say our vows in the chapel of the very same Presbyterian church where his sister married. After the ceremony, my mother teases Bill with a smile, saying, "You checked out everything but her teeth." He had won her over, and they were the best of friends for the next 45 years.

Our movie saga continues. Bill and I have been together "for better or worse" for 55 years now.

*With my new husband Bill at our wedding*

# Gleaning

We had just moved from Paso Robles to Templeton in 2018. I hadn't been over to the old house in two weeks. Unfortunately, a heat wave had done its damage to the fruit trees: one side of each apricot was brown and freckled, its skin starting to pucker from the heat, while the underside still had a tinge of unripe green. Guess I won't enter these in the county fair this year, I told myself. The challenge of turning these sad-looking apricots into useable food sparked my interest, as always, so I rolled up my sleeves and went in search of my old canning jars.

In 1981, I was working as a part-time secretary at the United Presbyterian Church in Nampa, Idaho, and I had done my own share of foraging for food when our cupboards at home looked bare. My husband, the country boy, had planted a large garden in the backyard. Our division of labor was firmly established. He was responsible for crop maintenance through harvest when our two young girls would help uproot anything still standing. Then it was up to me, the city girl, to preserve our bounty by canning, drying, and freezing.

But the garden alone was not enough to get us by. In the summer, we found fallen fruit to gather from under the neighbors' trees. In the fall my husband went pheasant hunting, and in the winter he endured ice-fishing. He even brought home castoff potatoes from work at the potato processing plant to round out our evening meals. I understood what it was like—not knowing when our food supply would run out and whether we could make it to the next paycheck.

The back-to-the-land movement of the 1970s asked people to become more self-sufficient by growing their own food, whether in community gardens or by living off the land. The Gleaning Cooperative of Caldwell County, Idaho, was part of that grassroots movement. This supplemental food program was created to reduce food waste and provide fresh food to those in need. In that spirit of community, I became a gleaning coordinator.

In this new role, I arranged for groups of volunteers to meet and harvest food that otherwise would have gone to waste. Calls came in to the church where I worked from various farms and ranches. Corn stalks, bent by a recent hailstorm, could not be harvested by machine. Volunteers drove out to the field and picked more than a thousand pounds of corn that day to be distributed to low-income families.

When we heard that plums, harvested and later found to be too large for factory canning specifications, were going to be buried in a large pit next to the processing plant, we retrieved and distributed a huge truckload of fruit. Windfall apples were my favorite—fallen fruit that had just hit the ground and was not damaged. On windy days after gleaning and canning most of my share, I remember making apple pies to share with everyone else in my neighborhood. My neighbors were surprised and happy to receive the treat, and I was happy to share my bounty with them.

When I studied at U.C. Berkeley in the early 70s, my field of interest was community nutrition. Back then, supplemental food programs were supported by federal funding and community activism. Thanks to Bobby Kennedy and others in public office, the school breakfast program took its place alongside the school lunch program in 1966, and the WIC program was created for women with infants and children under the age of five in 1974. Agricultural scientists were looking at ways to increase crop yield by developing hybrid grains in the spirit of feeding the world, not feeding corporate profits.

But by the time I left Idaho and returned to college in 1983, both federal and state budget cuts heavily targeted social programs. Federally supported community nutrition programs were pared down to their elemental core, and most were on the verge of disappearing. Seeing a future need for more nutrition services within the medical community, I changed my major to clinical nutrition. I switched from helping hungry people eat enough to helping obese people eat less.

In 2018, when I had preserved most of the apricots I harvested, they stood like eight colorful sentinels in shiny glass quart jars on the shelves of my pantry. I felt a sense of satisfaction, knowing we had food stored for the next few months. Although I can now afford to buy food at the grocery store whenever I need to, I still remember how it felt to worry about not having enough. I made two cobblers with the rest of the fruit, sharing one with family and the other with friends at church.

I was fortunate to be able to use the skills I developed in the 1970s to give back to my community. Back then I was part of a grassroots movement that fostered community spirit. Now, during a time of political divisiveness, we need a gleaning spirit to bring us together again.

*The fruit of my labor*

# Shall We Dance?

*By Eileen O'Grady*

Poised at the edge of the dance floor in my red cheetah top and sequined skirt, I gripped Dan's hand. The master of ceremonies introduced us, describing our dance as an aerobic routine that reflected all the joys and pitfalls of marriage. The 250 people in the ballroom laughed, and I breathed a little easier.

A few years earlier, when my husband and I retired, we moved to a small town on California's Central Coast. I volunteered at a food pantry and joined the library board; he assisted seniors with their taxes and served on local planning commissions. He played tennis; I took dance classes. We met many new people; we seldom encountered each other. I had hoped for a retirement that would knit a new pattern for our relationship—without the demands of parenting and professional obligations. Our new activities only reinforced our separate lives.

My dream relationship fluttered on the horizon when I was invited to perform in a hometown version of "Dancing with the Stars," a fundraiser for our local library. If Dan became my partner, we'd be working together. We had taken ballroom dance classes before, but I hesitated. What would happen if he said yes? He agreed, and our new journey began.

Recalling our successful rumba lessons, I contacted Frank, a local Latin dance instructor. Frank quickly vetoed rumba as "not showy enough," and suggested samba or salsa. Dan chose salsa. Salsa? Really? Rumba is cool, slow, and romantic; salsa is hot, fast, and sexy. Even Frank sounded uncertain; he mumbled something about complex steps.

We began our salsa lessons with the basic 1-2-3- hold-4 salsa step and then jumped into combinations. Learning the steps was like flirting on the dance floor—well, some of the time. A forceful leader, Frank was easy to follow. "You're doing salsa," he beamed. When I danced with Frank, I soared; with Dan, I stumbled along. Frank applauded each success, so we felt victorious.

Within a few weeks, we had learned the basics, so Frank selected music for our performance. Apart from an occasional "Ran-Kan-Kan," there were no lyrics—so helpful when you're learning choreography—and the pace was twice as fast as the "Salsa in English" tunes we practiced with at home. "You can do it," Frank said. Dan looked skeptical.

Could we remember the crossover steps in the proper sequence? Would the spins start and end on the beat? Dan rearranged our storage garage, so we'd have a larger space for practices. In the weeks that followed, we occasionally finished the first two sections of the dance without major mistakes. And when he twirled me, I could still see the green-eyed boy I'd fallen for in third grade. We were on a salsa honeymoon.

The honeymoon crashed when Frank unveiled the final minute of choreography—a chain of complex sequences and flourishing final moves. We walked through the new steps in class. We tried—and failed—to recall them at home. Was it step right, turn left? Or step left, turn right?

Did we face each other before or after the spin? And exactly which type of spin was it? Now the event was just weeks off. The final section of choreography, so crisp and clear on paper, blurred on the dance floor, threatening even our mastery of the earlier parts.

I was always ready to practice. To me salsa was sexy steps and hot music; to engineer Dan it was following a blueprint. I wanted salsa to bring us closer; he wanted it to be over. Our performance was only a couple of weeks off now. Our dance adventure was sinking, threatened by our differing outlooks, as well as our choreography. "Ran-Kan-Kan" had become our death knell.

"This dance is just too hard for us," Dan complained.

"There's no whining in dance," I responded angrily. Yes, the dance was challenging. But we could master it we practiced enough. After a day-long respite, we returned to the dance floor, bloodied, but not quite broken. As we listened with fresh ears, we began to hear subtle changes in the music's tempo and instrumentation that cued the later steps. Gradually our feet slid into the new footwork. We ignored minor missteps. Growing more confident, we re-shaped the final poses.

Over the next few days, we glided through the first third of the dance, then the second third, then all the way to the end. I held my breath. Could we do it again? As he grew more confident, my aging Tom Hanks became Antonio Banderas—swaying hips, flashing arms, and smoldering looks. Where had my reluctant husband gone? Who was this exciting new person?

On the night of the event, I chatted nervously with friends at our table. Our son David and his fiancée Michelle had driven up from L.A. to support us. When the program began, we stood near the entrance to the ballroom. The audience disappeared as we listened for the opening staccato beats of our music. We sprang into the flirtatious first sequence, then moved into spot turns and twirls as the tempo quickened. Two minutes into the dance we reached the tricky sweetheart pattern where we twirl together and apart rapidly. After we each soloed across the dance floor, we partnered to complete a flamenco spin and final poses. The happy sound of applause greeted us as the music ended and we bowed to the audience.

*Dan and I performed a challenging salsa in 2013*

Because so many friends supported us, we raised $28,000 for the library, and we were awarded first place. A few days later our costumed photo appeared on the front page of our local newspaper. For a few weeks, we floated on a post-performance bubble as people congratulated us. Our learning-process bruises faded further when we shared our videotaped performance. After all, the product looked polished.

Despite our 15 minutes of fame, alas, no shiny new relationship emerged. Ours was still the familiar saga of two very different people who trust each other enough to learn new and challenging ways to partner. And maybe that's enough.

# Where I Belonged

By *Shirley Summers*

I was sitting outside a counselor's office waiting to enroll in my first year at Diablo Valley College. I wondered how I had ever gotten to this place. Most of my teachers did not expect me to go to college. No one in my immediate family had ever been to college, and I had never even entertained the idea of going. That was something that smart kids did, and they had good grades in all their classes, not just a few.

My high school grades could not have gotten me into a four-year college. Only my math and science grades were good—mostly As and a few Bs. As I waited, I thought about what my mother said, "Why don't you just try junior college and see how you like it?"

I sat waiting for the counselor, not having a clue what I would do if this did not suit me. I could not stand the cacophony of sounds made by the business machines or the typewriters when I picked my friend Betty up for lunch after her business classes. Betty liked those classes, but the sound of the machines made me want to pull out my hair.

I suppose I could have gotten married. I had a boyfriend who was a year older than I was. We dated and went steady throughout high school. He joined the Marines right after his high school graduation. He had asked me to marry him, but if I did that, I would become just like my mother. I did not want to be my mother; I wanted to be me.

Although my mother did not get married until she was 25 and worked for eight years before giving birth, she had liked business classes. She became a stay-at-home mother after I was born until I was 16, and then she returned to work in a job using business machines. I liked my mother, and she had a good life, but I wanted something different. I had always wanted to make my own decisions and create my own identity—whatever that might be.

I heard my name being called and knew that it was my turn to talk to the counselor. As I walked into the office, I could feel my heart pounding. I was sure she would ask me what I was doing here. I had no idea what I would say. Maybe I should tell her what I was thinking—that I was probably wasting her time. I imagined she would see that I was not smart enough to go to college, and then she would send me on my way. I would leave her office with no goals, aspirations or plans.

"How long have you lived in Pleasant Hill?" she began. "What do you like to do for fun?"

It was not what I expected.

"What do you like about math and science?" I tried to explain why math and science appealed to me.

She spent a long time just looking from one piece of paper on her desk to another piece of paper on her desk: my high school grades and my placement test scores. Then she stopped to look at me. As we sat in silence, my hands were sweating, and I wanted to get up and leave. I tried to look calm.

When the counselor began to write, I could not see what was on the paper. I thought the worst. When she finished, she talked about the classes she had assigned me to. She said, "I can see that you really like math and science."

"Yes. I do." I responded.

"I have given you a physical science class and a live science class. That way you will have two classes that suit your interests. I think you will enjoy the logic class too; it is very much like math. I expect you will do well here at Diablo Valley College."

She handed me a class schedule with 19 1/2 semester units. I did not know what a student's first semester schedule should look like; later I learned it was a heavy class load. I was enrolled in Chemistry 1A and Zoology 1A, both of which had six hours of labs a week in addition to lectures. Besides the logic class she mentioned, she had enrolled me in psychology, English, and ballroom dancing.

My first two years of college amazed me. Doing real chemistry was so much more interesting than high school chemistry. Zoology was so much better in college too; we did not have to work in groups. I had my own animal to dissect, so I could work at my own speed. I was so attached to my dogfish shark that I took it home to dissect it more completely. My parents were not thrilled. "You cannot keep that dead animal that smells of formaldehyde here in the house. It has to be in the garage," they said. So, bundled up in my coat, I sat in the garage while I completed my dissection.

In my logic class, I was introduced to syllogisms and deductive logic. Most of all, my excitement in learning stayed with me as I took other general education classes. One day my social psychology professor said to the class, "I think everyone should take a course in economics, so that you understand how the government works."

I took an economics class, and then another one, until that was my major at the university. In economics I once again dissected a situation. I particularly enjoyed theory and econometrics. I finally realized that I belonged in college when the head of the economics department asked me to participate in honors classes. Later I was invited to join the student section of Omicron Delta Epsilon, an internationally known honor society in the field of economics. I held onto their journals for a long time and periodically took them out to look at them, just to prove to myself that I belonged.

*My graduation with an MSW from U.C. Berkeley in 1995*

That day in the counselor's office at Diablo Valley College took me on a journey that I will always be grateful for. I used deductive logic and syllogistic thinking whenever I wrote reports for the court—both while I was working in Child Welfare Services and later as a therapist writing treatment plans to help clients reach their goals. I was looking at the components of a situation and constructing a plan to

*Triumphs*

facilitate a logical outcome, just as I did many years ago in my math and science classes.

# The Audition

*By Myra Lathrop*

"**M**yra and William," the assistant choreographer announced loudly through her microphone. My heart was pounding; my legs felt weak and wobbly. William, my salsa dance partner of almost two years, took my hand and led me out to the studio dance floor. With perfect dance posture and anxious smiles, we took our first steps to a Tito Puente mambo from the 1950s.

Our paths first crossed in 1989 at one of the many salsa dance clubs in L.A. William was tall and handsome with jet black hair and dark eyes; he was a sharp dresser and a smooth and elegant dancer. The first time he asked me to dance, we both knew we were a good partnership.

But when he called to tell me about the audition, my response was "no way."

"Why not?" he demanded.

"Because we aren't good enough. And we're older. (I was 41; he was 36.) You know those young Latino professional dancers from the movie *Salsa* are our competition. We don't stand a chance."

"We're doing it," he answered firmly. I was positive that we would look ridiculous, but I acquiesced; I did not want to lose one of the best salseros in L.A. as a partner.

The auditions were held at the Debbie Reynolds Dance Studio in North Hollywood. Along with fifty other couples, we were auditioning for roles as principal dancers in a movie called *Mambo Kings*, starring Armand Assante and Antonio Banderas. This was the third day of auditions, open to both professionals and non-professionals.

Because we were the second to the last couple to perform, we had watched most of the other pairs cut loose with their best spins, dips, lifts, and fancy footwork. We had been told that we needed to dance on "two," or the offbeat, as the producer wanted the dancing to reflect the style popular at The Palladium in NYC in the early 1950s. Most of us in L.A. had learned to dance on "one."

Our dances were taped, so that the choreographers could study us in more detail later. Michael Peters, the man who created most of Michael Jackson's videos, was the main choreographer.

Half way through our audition, I felt William ramp up his energy. His lead became forceful and tense. I smiled at him, hoping he would lighten up. He responded by directing me into a series of spins that were so rapid, I almost tripped over my own feet. At least we were able to dance on the dreaded "two." By the time the dance ended, we were both soaked in perspiration.

Out of breath and thirsty, we walked off the floor to join the other dancers. Despite receiving compliments and pats on the back, I knew we would not make the cut. They only needed twelve couples; I could not imagine we would be one of them.

"I never want to do that again," I announced to William on our drive home.

"We did great. Why are you so negative?" he asked. I pouted in silence the rest of the way.

About two weeks later, I received a call at the dental office where I was the office manager. Kim, one of the assistant choreographers, introduced herself.

"Congratulations, Myra! You and William have been chosen to be dancers in the film."

"I'm sorry, Kim, but I can't afford to take two weeks off to be an extra; it just won't pay enough."

"No, you will be principal dancers. You'll earn union scale with overtime."

"You're kidding!" I shrieked. "I can't believe it! Are you sure?"

Laughing, she replied, "Be ready for long hours and lots of hard work. Rehearsals at the studio begin next week, eight hours a day, for three days. Then we shoot downtown at the old Ambassador Hotel Ballroom. Make-up and hair begin at 5:30 a.m."

I thanked her and hung up; then I called William. My hands were so shaky, I could barely dial. "We did it!" I shouted into the receiver.

He already knew. "I told you there was nothing to worry about. Why were you so uptight?" His cool demeanor didn't fool me; I knew he was as excited as I was.

The two weeks of rehearsal and shooting the film were more difficult than Kim could possibly have conveyed on the phone. I felt exhausted and exhilarated every day. Dance was such a contrast to my daily job which was filled with talking to patients and juggling appointments and insurance details. And, unlike the nerve-wracking audition, dancing our hearts out in front of the camera came easily and smoothly. What had I been so afraid of?

When *Mambo Kings* premiered a year later in Westwood Village, William and I attended, along with other dancers and cast members. Although the director was an ex-mambo dancer himself, many of the dance segments wound up on the cutting room floor. We barely recognized ourselves in the routines that remained. We were disappointed, but not discouraged.

*William and I posing on the set of Mambo Kings, 1991*

A few months later William called to tell me there was an audition for a Miller Lite commercial for Spanish television. Instantly my stomach contracted, and my pulse began to race.

"Do we have to?" I whined.

"Yes!" he replied emphatically.

# Valentine's Day, 1994

*By Martha Staib*

In the 1990s, I often heard that single women over 40 were more likely to be killed by terrorists than to get married. That belief was later proven to be false, but at the time, it felt very real to me. My life had settled into a routine of working as a dietitian at the local state hospital and guiding my two daughters, Jennifer and Carleen, through their sometimes-turbulent teen years. I was not keen to start another relationship. Atascadero was a small, family-oriented town with not many single prospects anyway, but occasionally I landed a date and enjoyed an evening out on the town.

During my single-parenting years, the girls developed a checklist for my handful of potential suitors. They refined it with each new candidate and scored accordingly.

1. No bell-bottom pants (Guess that was the tall psych tech from the hospital);

2. No evidence of baldness or thinning hair (Wow—looking back, they ALL were bald or had thinning hair);

3. No aversion to Boise, our household cat (I was not a cat person, but the girls felt their cat needed to be acknowledged by my visitors.)

4. No smacking sounds when eating bananas (O.K., so that turned out not to be a deal-breaker.)

In 1993, I started dating Ron when he separated from his wife and moved north of the Cuesta Grade. I had worked with him at the state hospital for years and saluted him during our U.S. Army Reserve weekend drills in Ventura. He had light brown hair and a charming lopsided smile.

By then Jennifer had graduated from high school and moved out, leaving the dating checklist to Carleen. Apparently Ron scored high enough on his initial visit to allow me to continue dating him.

In early February of 1994, Ron asked if I would like to go skiing on Valentine's Day weekend. "Gosh, that sounds like fun," I said, not sure about the skiing but eager to go anywhere on an adventure with another adult.

Later, I did admit that I had not been on a pair of skis since I was about nine years old—when I skied on a frozen lake, using a rope tow. "No problem," he replied. "There are plenty of beginner runs at Sierra Summit." And so we packed up and headed out for our first weekend date. There was plenty of snow; the skies were clear. Who could ask for more?

On Saturday morning we drove east through Fresno and up to the mountain resort. The day was clear and cool as we hit the slopes for a sunny afternoon of skiing. It took me a while to get used to the feel of the rental poles, boots, and skis, but I did O.K. on the bunny slope. We enjoyed a delicious steak dinner at the Sierra Summit Inn. We felt the stress of working in a maximum-security mental hospital begin to fade away as we shared stories with each other in the warm glow of candlelight. A fire burned in the nearby stone fireplace. After dinner we finished our evening with a stroll along the outdoor deck, appreciating the stillness of the mountain pines and feeling relaxed in each other's company.

On Sunday Ron checked out the higher mountain trails while I took a ski lesson and progressed to the T-bar run, staggering and falling when I let go of the bar, but finally getting the hang of it. Late in the afternoon, I agreed to take the chair lift with Ron part way up the mountain. Once I settled onto the lift chair, I managed to control my fear of heights by looking straight ahead. I told myself, "Don't look down! Don't look down!" In the distance, I could see the short landing area that sloped sharply down the hill. When my feet touched the ground, I shuffled off the lift, staggered forward, lost my balance, and fell to the ground. One knee twisted sharply against the skis, and pain radiated up my leg.

Ron had already hopped off the chair and maneuvered his way to the bottom turn of the slope. When he looked back, I was lying on the ground, moaning and angrily pounding the snow with my fist. I struggled as I tried to get out of the way of the newly-disembarked skiers behind me; some barely missed me as they skied by, yelling, "Get out of the way!"

The chair-lift operator finally stopped the line, and a ski patrol volunteer rolled me onto a rescue sled. He skied down the black diamond trail, pulling me behind on the bobbing sled. Ron followed us on another trail. We all met at the bottom of the mountain where I was examined at the first aid station and given a knee brace and crutches. My romantic ski weekend was over.

Ron remained calm when our weekend didn't go as planned; he helped me to see the bright side of the situation by telling me funny stories on the drive home, so I wouldn't feel so embarrassed. He arranged his work schedule to escort me to my doctor's appointment and later to drive

me home after my MRI and orthoscopy. We would need those same qualities again to face the complications of dating as work colleagues—and later when we married and blended our families together.

When I arrived home after the ski trip, I told Carleen she could toss her dating checklist. I had written my own, and Ron had passed with flying colors.

*Ron and I at our wedding reception in 1998*

# We Were Fierce

*By Eileen O'Grady*

"We were fierce," Sue said to me, her brown eyes shining as she recalled our experiences on the library's fundraising committee. We were walking out of the conference room at the Atascadero Library as she spoke.

I recalled our weekly meetings from 2009 through 2013. We both arrived early at the room attached to the former library on Morro Road. We unlocked the door and switched on fluorescent lights in the still-dingy room. Then we dragged mismatched sticky tables together to create a makeshift conference table. A new Atascadero Library with a dedicated conference room was just a dream.

"I'll never forget what you said when I joined the committee," Sue continued.

"What did I say?"

"You asked me if I was sure I wanted to do this."

I don't remember saying that, but I suppose I did. I wanted the most dedicated and talented people I knew to be on that committee. By the time Sue joined us, about six months after our campaign was announced, we had donned our battle gear. Most of us were retired professional women with decades of experience in business, social services, and education, but little experience in fundraising.

We had launched our campaign efforts at a café at the south end of town. When our fundraising consultant asked who was leading the meeting, the Friends of the Library President replied, "Eileen." I did not expect that role, but I didn't resist. For several months I had encouraged our board to commit to a new library. We felt the chill of the Great

114 *Triumphs*

Recession, but county matching funds and the support of our county supervisors would vanish if we hesitated.

In addition to raising funds, we faced the challenge of working with the county in an uneasy partnership. The county never published agendas for our joint meetings or provided minutes afterwards. County bureaucrats who attended meetings changed monthly. And, with no agenda, we could never prepare beforehand. We could only react.

The library project had now become my baby, so I had to learn to represent our community at those meetings. I began slowly, asking questions and offering alternatives. By the time we met with the project architect, I had found my voice. About midway through the meeting, the architect looked around the table filled with county staffers and Friends of the Library volunteers and asked, "How are decisions made?" I imagine he saw us as an unwieldy group that could stymie the design process.

"This is a county library," the library director replied, deepening his voice and puffing out his chest. "So, any decisions will be made by the county."

I had to say something, but what? I assumed my most saccharine voice. "We really don't expect any problems," I began. "But if the Friends of the Library board is not satisfied with the direction of this project, all fundraising will cease." No one uttered a word, but we had staked our position.

Sometimes new members to our committee inspired the rest of us. That was certainly true of our financial wizard, a semi-retired CPA. Marguerite created the pristine financial statements and the pastel pie charts we needed to convince large donors. At meetings with the county, our blond bulldog scrutinized all the financial information, ensuring that our contributions were protected.

Not everyone had her moxie. "But I've never done this before," one volunteer whined when she was asked to complete a task.

"We're all doing things we've never done before," I replied. I don't imagine that Sue, our committee secretary, thought she would also coordinate a garden tour in her neighborhood, a fundraiser that raised thousands of dollars. I suspect Liz, our grant-writer, never planned to lead a children's event. And none of us could have envisioned the annual dance event we created, a benefit so popular and successful that it outlived the campaign.

Finding grants during a recession was nearly impossible, but Liz captured the attention of a local foundation with thorough responses to their 34-question application. The second phase was an interview he would conduct with the team. Since several of our key members were not available, I needed to represent us.

"What professional fundraising training has your group had?" the foundation president asked as the meeting began. I told him about the workshops we had attended at the California Library Association and the fundraising consultant we had hired for several months.

"What have you accomplished so far?"

"We already had almost a million dollars in the bank before the project began," I said. "In our first year we developed one $100,000 donor and a growing cadre of $1,000-$5,000 donors." Their names were listed on posters on the adjacent tables. I mentioned Atascadero: Dancing with Our Stars, our fundraising event that had netted $25,000 its first year.

"You need to recruit more large donors," he replied. I nodded in agreement. Finding large donors was one of our biggest challenges.

"What obstacles have you overcome?" he asked.

I described the deed restriction that prevented the sale of the current library property. When county efforts failed, a county attorney called and asked me to contact the heirs of the donor who had restricted the deed. I told him how I drafted an email explaining our community's desire to relocate the library in a large, unfinished downtown building. The deed restriction was removed the next day.

"I dealt with those heirs on another project," he replied, smiling. And suddenly the interview was over. A few weeks later we received the $100,000 we had requested. Working together, we had navigated a tricky maze. And now we had a second $100,000 donor.

We invited our large donors and other community supporters to a celebration in the still-unfinished building that could become the new

Atascadero Library. We stared at the bare framing and envisioned the possibilities—a conference room here, a community room there, ample space for children and adults. As we sipped punch and ate cupcakes, one of our larger donors, a retired school librarian, promised another $100,000 donation. The recession still raged, but dedicated donors had brightened a bleak landscape.

Some of us spoke to groups. Some approached individuals. Others visited local businesses to request sponsorships or auction items. When one person succeeded, we all relished her victory. We had become a relay team that could navigate even the highest hurdles. If someone stumbled, we lifted her up and never looked back. We added more books to the stack of books that marked our progress on the large sign near the new library. Then we photographed our donors in front of it. "It's a team effort," I reminded everyone who commented on our success. "You can join us."

The fundraising campaign lasted four years. Near the end, we were $30,000 short of our goal, and the deadline was fast approaching. Then one of our team members stepped forward to offer us a personal loan she had secured. We overcame another obstacle and met our deadline.

*The Atascadero Library on opening day, June 2014*

On a clear summer morning in June 2014, the library was ready to open. I arrived early and photographed the exterior of the newly painted building. Inside everything was fresh and attractive—from the decorative tree that honored our larger donors to the artist-designed silk banner that gently rotated in the lobby. Then scores of adults and children arrived to celebrate with hot dogs and cake as we opened the doors of the cheerful new Atascadero Library.

We, the members of the fundraising team, quietly removed our fierce masks and slipped back into our familiar roles—retired professionals, community volunteers, grandmothers. We look like everyone else when we enter the library to check out a book or attend a meeting. But the library campaign had transformed us. We were fierce once; we could be fierce again.

Made in the USA
Las Vegas, NV
04 March 2021